ADVANCED SPORT DIVING

BS·AC

The British Sub-Aqua Club

Stanley Paul

London

Stanley Paul & Co. Ltd

An imprint of Random House (UK) Ltd
20 Vauxhall Bridge Road, London SW1V 2SA

Random House Australia (Pty) Ltd
20 Alfred Street, Milsons Point, Sydney, NSW 2061

Random House New Zealand Ltd
18 Poland Road, Glenfield, Auckland 10, New Zealand

First published 1990

New edition 1992

Set in 9 on 10pt Rockwell Light

Printed and bound in Great Britain by
Butler & Tanner Ltd, Frome and London

British Library Cataloguing in Publication Data
Advanced sport diving.
    1. Recreations: Underwater diving
    I. British Sub-Aqua Club
    1. 1797.2'3

    ISBN 0-09-177265-6

Also available
Sport Diving
Seamanship for Divers
Safety and Rescue for Divers
Snorkelling for All

Contents

ADVANCED
SPORT DIVING

BS·AC

This Manual is dedicated to the memory of DAVE SHAW

Decompression Diving

Underwater Techniques

Specialist Diving

Expedition Diving

Foreword

Although diving is categorized as a sport, it often sits very uncomfortably in that classification. It is only the fact that sports divers pursue the activity in their leisure time that overlaps with conventional sporting activities. Indeed, diving is often described as merely a means of transport, which then allows the diver to pursue other activities, having gained access to the underwater world.

Whether it is for the sheer pleasure of being able to swim freely and explore underwater, or the pursuit of another interest such as ecology or archaeology, divers seem to share one common trait. This is a natural thirst for knowledge of the underwater realm and understanding of the effect that penetrating it has on their physiology.

This book is designed to extend that awareness, both theoretically and practically. It contains a wealth of detailed knowledge and describes practical techniques to benefit all divers, whatever their underwater interests.

Whilst it intends to increase both the breadth and depth of knowledge, it has an important aim that such knowledge will also increase the safety of the diver. The more we understand about our sport, the safer we should be in pursuing it and, ultimately, the more enjoyment it will offer us.

Deric Ellerby
BSAC National Diving Officer

Acknowledgements

The British Sub-Aqua Club gratefully acknowledges the efforts of the following persons who have contributed to this publication.

Editors:
Deric Ellerby
Mike Holbrook
Gordon Longworth

Contributors:
Mike Busuttili
Deric Ellerby
Mike Holbrook
Dave Shaw
Mike Todd
Barry Winfield

Dive Planning

Dive Planning

Dive planning is perhaps the most important phase in the structure of any dive, and it is useful at this point to outline the factors to be considered. All dive plans should take into account the following points:

a. The numbers and level of experience of the diving group.
b. The means of transport to the dive site by either land or sea.
c. The presence of any tidal streams and their prediction.
d. The likelihood of poor weather conditions and their prediction.
e. The time needed to travel to the site and the time required for fixing the exact location.
f. Decompression/air consumption calculations.
g. The predicted actions to be followed in any emergency situation.

The numbers and level of experience of any diving group obviously affect the choice of dive site and need to be built into dive planning. It is inadvisable to have large groups of divers all in the water at the same time, and splitting them into two waves is much more manageable. This inevitably takes more time, and in those parts of the world with a small tidal stream window numbers may have to be restricted on any particular site if all are to enjoy slack-water diving. Levels of experience may differ among the dive group, and any plan must have a workable ratio of experienced divers or instructors to accompany the less experienced on their dives. Too many diving accidents have occurred as a result of novice divers being put into situations which they did not have the experience to cope with. Personnel will certainly influence the choice and location of the dive being planned.

Transporting divers safely to the site either by land or sea is part of any successful dive plan. All methods of transport are fairly predictable in terms of average speed accomplished in normal conditions. Most travel on land is by road vehicle. Good dive plans will compromise between economy, in terms of how many bodies and how much equipment can be carried in any vehicle, and the comfort of those travelling. Travelling by sea will either be by fast-planing boats or the more leisurely pace of displacement hulls. The latter, of course, vary in size and degrees of comfort. Whatever type of boat is used, adequate travelling time must be built into the plan, with due allowances being made in terms of slippage time for the unforeseen. This may include mechanical breakdown or unpredicted weather conditions such as sea fog.

In many dive locations throughout the world tidal streams are either non-existent or are so weak that they fail to be a planning factor when deciding whether dives are possible or not. In other parts of the world, diving is impossible unless the slack-water period between tides is chosen, and to try to dive in such a tidal stream is uncomfortable, impossible and foolhardy. The use of tide tables and nautical charts allows accurate prediction of slack-water periods in most parts of the world. The wise planner, however, will realize that these are only predictions and that local conditions such as extreme low or high air pressure, or strong winds, can affect exact timings.

Weather prediction is not usually a problem in those parts of the world with a predictable climate. There are many dive locations where local boatmen will not put out to sea if the wind creates half-metre waves, being content to wait for complete calm conditions. In other locations half-metre waves would be regarded as quite calm and perfectly suited for diving activities. Although we have this contrast, it is prudent for any dive planner to take account of weather conditions. It is of little use to arrive on site in a boat with all personnel suffering severe symptoms of *mal de mer* because no account had been taken of wind direction and strength.

Time needed to travel to a dive site has already been mentioned, but an additional allowance must always be given for locating the exact site once in the general area. This may not be a problem if the site is well known or marked in any way. If not, it is surprising how much time can be spent hovering over a depth sounder waiting for the trace to alter.

Decompression and air consumption calculations obviously vary according to the depth/duration of the planned dive. Although this is part of any pre-dive brief, it is important that some consideration is given to it during the planning stages to enable divers to acquire adequate capacity cylinders and to ensure that any extra equipment, such as shotlines and buoys, is carried.

No one would wish for any diving accident or emergency, but the unpredictable does happen and to plan your reaction to it may influence a potential dive plan. It is, for example, very unwise to plan prolonged periods of repetitive deep diving because of the increased risk of decompression sickness. To plan the same in areas where recompression facilities may be many hours, even days, away is foolhardy.

Figure 1 Dive marshal briefing students

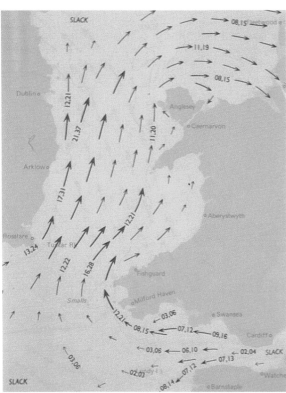

Figure 2 Local tidal predictions

Figure 3 Sea conditions unsuitable for diving

Figure 4 Sea fog can descend quickly and without warning

Dive Marshalling

The dive marshal is the key figure in the organization of any diving activity. Diving clubs throughout the world appoint their most experienced and responsible individuals to take on this crucial role. Commercial dive schools and dive shops have experienced professional instructors in the same role.

What skills and expertise are called for in the successful dive marshal? The BSAC diving manual *Sport Diving* lists the activities and responsibilities of the dive marshal. For the smooth running of the dive, the dive marshal becomes manager or co-ordinator of several activities.

A successful manager delegates responsibility to those capable of fulfilling the role given. An unsuccessful manager tries to do everything himself, does not think ahead, or gives people jobs they are incapable of carrying out.

The dive marshal needs to enjoy his own diving, and can only do this if an effective plan is formulated, adequate time allowed for travel, for the diving itself, and for the unexpected. The latter necessitates the need for some time slippage, which often becomes part of the day and can be disastrous if it is not allowed and planned for. In tidal waters the tide will not wait for late arrivals.

As mentioned above, a dive marshal is a dive manager and to manage effectively some delegation of responsibility is usually necessary. Conditions and modes of diving operation vary throughout the world, and there is no standard procedure or method of diving. The British diving scene has traditionally involved other skills as well as those connected with the actual dive. These include boat launching and retrieval, boat handling, navigation and position fixing at the dive site. In other parts of the world nobody is allowed to drive a boat unless they have a licence or other relevant qualification, and these skills do not directly involve the dive marshal other than ensuring the dive plan is fully understood by all concerned. In most commercial dive operations the diving will be organized by a professional supervisor or divemaster, who handles all the details. All the diver has to do is to turn up for the dive. The dive pairings are made, choice of site predetermined and all precautions for diving safety established. This type of diving is very much a package, and may not appeal to those who are used to planning their own diving activities.

Regardless of the dive location there are several tasks which are standard in the running of any dive.

One of the standard diving recommendations, except in specialized circumstances, is that diving is conducted in buddy pairs. Many commercial operators in clearwater locations may not strictly adhere to this procedure, since an instructor or dive guide will lead a group of divers, perhaps up to six in number, and then operate in a follow-my-leader fashion. Such operations are not recommended if the group are novices, for obvious reasons, but can work for experienced divers who merely wish to be shown around. Even so, the wise dive marshal will buddy people up so that each diver knows and understands who he may be responsible for in the water.

In normal buddy diving the wise dive marshal will know the experience and preferences of those under his charge. A common-sense procedure is to place together divers with similar cylinder capacities and breathing rates.

With the use of the BSAC '88 decompression tables the pairing of divers with the same current tissue code is another consideration. This will become more significant after the first dive of the day, and will also become important if pairs of divers are broken up for later dives. The observant dive marshal also places together people with similar kitting-up speeds, for obvious reasons. Staggered entries in diving waves will avoid having all the divers kitting-up at once, or everyone trying to get down the anchor rope at the same time. More importantly, from the safety point of view, there will be no requirement to pick up all the surfacing divers at the same time. Many divers have their own buddy, usually a close friend, and it is unwise to try to separate these pairs against their will. Decompression computers have an increasing role to play in dive planning, and due regard must be made for their use when marshalling a dive.

Dive marshals are responsible for keeping an accurate dive log (see Figure 5), which must also include space for both a surfacing time and current tissue code in order to work out decompression requirements on the BSAC '88 tables. When the dive marshal is in the water, another responsible person must be tasked with record-keeping.

Further responsibilities may include organization of cylinder filling, refuelling boats, provision of refreshment and shelter, and liaison with the coastguard. The final list compiled by the dive marshal will reflect the needs of his specific group of divers and must be best suited to providing safe, enjoyable diving for them, wherever they may be in the world.

In summary, remember the following golden rules for managing a successful dive:

delegation to competent helpers
forward planning
attention to detail

Common sense underlies all of the above.

BRITISH SUB·AQUA CLUB   DIVE MARSHALLING SLATE

DATE _____   DIVE SITE _____

SLACK _____   WEATHER _____

START DIVING _____   _____

END DIVING _____   SEA _____

MARSHAL _____   DEPUTY MARSHAL _____

BS·AC

NAME	QUAL'N	CURRENT TISSUE CODE	AIR	TIME DOWN	TIME UP	MAX DEPTH	STOPS		DIVE TIME	SURFACE CODE	COMMENTS
							1st	2nd			

Figure 5 BSAC dive marshalling slate

Dive Leading

Dive leading is a major responsibility on any dive and may require the ability to make split-second decisions. The role of dive leader varies according to geographical location. At one extreme we have the dive guide in warm clear-water locations who may have up to six divers under his control, possibly with someone else acting as a sheepdog at the end, keeping in line any stragglers from the group. At the other extreme we have the buddy pair who may be diving in such poor visibility that a buddy line is required to ensure they keep contact.

Whatever the situation, the leader is the one who makes decisions during the dive and is the one given the responsibility by the dive marshal for its successful conclusion. Many experienced buddies dive only together, and over the years build up a diving empathy with regard to each other's activities and location. Even though they might be out of visual contact, they know where their buddy is and feel safe in each other's company. Other situations will see an inexperienced diver having to be restrained from darting off in all directions, like an eager greyhound on a lead, or constantly swimming above or to the side of the leader's field of vision. In the first situation the divers function as a team, and to deem someone the leader is somewhat irrelevant. The second situation, however, clearly needs strong leadership if both are to enjoy the dive.

When contemplating the art of successful dive leadership it is logical to split the dive into the briefing, the descent phase, the dive itself, the ascent and the debriefing.

The surface briefing should include all the important facets of the dive ahead. The mnemonic SEEDS as explained in the section on dive leadership in *Sport Diving* is a useful aid in ensuring an adequate briefing. This should cover all aspects of equipment, including the buddy check, the entry method into the water, the descent, and the dive itself. In a novice/experienced diver pairing the leader should enter the water first, in case the novice should have any difficulties. This may be important, for example, when jumping from a large boat for the first time.

The descent phase is particularly important for inexperienced divers in terms of regulating their breathing and eliminating any apprehension they may be feeling. There is nothing worse for the inexperienced diver than to arrive at the bottom breathless, perhaps with some water in his mask, and not having trimmed his buoyancy adequately, only to be expected to zoom off following his impatient leader. A shotline is a good aid in controlling the descent phase, especially in those areas in the world where visibility is limited and one cannot see the bottom. On arrival at the bottom a minute or two of orientation/breathing adjustment makes all the difference to the dive to follow.

In clear-water locations a free descent is both easy and acceptable practice.

Arguments sometimes rage about who should go down the shotline first. With experienced divers it matters little, but in a novice situation general advice would be to have the leader go first at not too fast a pace, constantly checking on the progress of his buddy. Some leaders wish their charges to go first, so they can go at their own pace and can be monitored from above. Problems can occur with this procedure when the novice descends too quickly due to overweighting, and divers have died in the past through becoming lost in this way. Many divers prefer to descend feet first, especially when wearing dry suits. A head-down descent in a dry suit can lead to air migration into the legs, which leads to lack of control and discomfort.

The dive itself depends on how familiar divers are with each other's speed and their dive-leading technique. As mentioned above, experienced divers will stay together without having to stress the point. With buddies who are unfamiliar or inexperienced it may be necessary to give clear instructions for them to swim on a particular side. While it is prudent to check on each other's welfare periodically during the dive there is nothing worse than having to repeatedly answer an OK signal every minute or so.

Experienced and successful dive leaders will plan their dive to arrive back at a predetermined place for the ascent. They will utilize all navigation/pilotage skills acquired over the years in order to achieve this.

The ascent phase of any dive is perhaps one area which has been ignored somewhat over the years, but is seen as critical in terms of current safe decompression practice. Ascents are normally carried out either after a predetermined time or when air supply is running low. Divers must allow adequate air for all stages of ascent, the amount varying according to the depth of the dive. The BSAC '88 decompression tables require strict control of ascent rates, and a stop at 6 metres in order to determine whether it is safe to ascend directly to the surface or not. In the past too many ascents have become uncontrolled near the surface, leading to many bends 'within the tables'. Dive leaders must ensure buoyancy is trimmed correctly, and that the ascent is fully controlled. Ascending up a line is obviously more easy to control, and will usually be necessary if decompression stops are required.

Figure 6 Dive leader showing a student a point of interest

Dive Location

The choice of diving location is of prime importance for the comfort and enjoyment of all divers.

The major consideration when choosing a site is to maximize the ease of access to the water and, just as importantly, the ease of egress or exit. What is an acceptable location under this consideration will, of course, vary according to the numbers, level of expertise of the divers, and other variables such as weather and tidal streams. Such variables mean that one must make different decisions about a particular location according to prevailing conditions. A 180° change of wind direction, for example, may make all the difference as to whether a site is suitable for diving or not.

A group of dive-fit experienced divers may well tackle a location which would be totally unsuitable for a group of novices. The sensible dive marshal will only consider dive locations which satisfy the safety demands of access and egress and must never put divers at risk by an unwise choice.

Remembering that enjoyment with safety is of prime importance, it is perhaps worth considering a few ground rules in choosing a suitable dive location for different levels of diver experience.

The novice diver is probably the most easily satisfied in terms of what is required from a dive. Many experienced divers become selective in their ambitions and choice of location, not being prepared to jump in anywhere for the sake of it. Having said that, the novice diver is the diver least familiar with his equipment, may be apprehensive and not as confident in carrying out the various roles to be filled throughout the dive. Novice divers do not need to be exposed to marginal or difficult conditions and a careful choice of location is required.

Working on the principle of progressive training, the first few open water dives should be an extension of pool or shallow water training. Many instructors will take their trainees on shore dives before exposing them to the wonders of boat diving, regarding this as a safer option as they can gradually acquire greater depth while swimming away from a beach. Many parts of the world do have sheltered and safe access points with relatively deep interesting dive locations close at hand. Other shore locations, however, are the worst possible places to take an inexperienced diver. Consider the boulder-strewn beach with occasional waves sweeping in, where the depth does not reach 2 metres until divers are perhaps 200 metres from the shore. In these conditions the novice, wearing bulky, heavy equipment has to walk backwards to find a depth where he may submerge without difficulty, and may well stumble over unseen rocks or seabed hollows, and once below the surface will initially see little else but sand being swept to and fro by wave action. By the time the divers reach open water they have already spent considerable time and energy, and some may well be out of breath. Many instructors insist that such shore locations are essential for first open water dives, when clearly they are not.

When faced with a choice, in the scenario just described, boat diving in a sheltered location is by far the wiser of the two choices. Diving from a boat avoids all the effort and inconvenience of gaining diving depths of water from a beach, as described above. Divers enter the water without having to swim great distances and a descent down the anchor allows control and orientation for the novice before the dive commences. Obviously, the procedure for getting back aboard the boat will need to be well understood by all members of the party.

The choice of suitable dive locations for more experienced divers may be wider, but will still need to be guided by common sense. Many experienced divers have got into difficulties by forgetting that, while gravity will help them enter the water, it is of no use when trying to leave it. Leaping into the water from a rocky headland, for example, is only to be recommended if one can be sure that exiting is possible. More than one suitable exiting point is recommended, but extreme care must be taken to ensure tidal streams, where they occur, do not make it impossible to reach such a point.

Winds are probably the most important influence on diving activities regardless of location. In the situation described directly above, common sense would say that such a location would be ruled out by an onshore wind of any strength. If your shore-based dive is to take place from an island, this will offer you a wider choice of safe locations as there will always be a lee shore.

Divers using boats have more freedom in that they may be able to find a lee shore, provided that conditions are not too marginal, on the journey to the site. Careful use of local charts, in conjunction with a knowledge of prevailing wind conditions, will allow the best choice of dive location for the comfort and ease of kitting up of the divers. However, such locations will not necessarily have the greatest underwater interest; it is all a matter of luck.

Figure 7 Poor choice for a shore dive – a boulder-strewn beach can make access difficult

Figure 8 A sandy beach can be a good choice for a shore dive, although the underwater visibility can deteriorate

Diving Conditions – British Isles

The diverse diving conditions around the coast of the British Isles reflect the variety of geology, scenery and weather which the region itself enjoys. The British Isles have been called the country of countries when a general description of scenery has been needed. Compare, for example, the mountain scenery of much of Scotland and Wales with the flat expanses of East Anglia or the rolling chalk 'downlands' of southern England. The variety of weather in the British Isles, where in any one week of the year, one can experience all four seasons, has a great influence on diving conditions. Tidal streams are semi-diurnal – that is to say that in any lunar day of twenty-four hours there are two high waters and two low waters – and are strong, especially on spring tides, notably in the English Channel and Irish Sea. When these tidal streams are funnelled through island groups, speeds of 7 knots can be experienced. In the open sea about 3 knots is the expected maximum.

Latitude plays a part in determining diving conditions, as it is only the moderating influence of the relatively warm seas surrounding the country which gives a climate less severe than one would expect. The British Isles lie roughly between 50 and 60 degrees north of the Equator. The Orkney Islands off the northern tip of Scotland share the same latitude as the southern tip of Greenland. The presence of the Gulf Stream, which brings warm water across the Atlantic from the Gulf of Mexico to sweep along the northwest coast of Scotland, ensures that not only do we not have the icebergs experienced in Greenland, but that palm trees can grow in the more sheltered places along the Scottish west coast. Although the northerly latitude does not give us the extremes of cold we might expect, it does have an effect on the hours of daylight. For example, in early June in the Orkneys, there are only about four hours of darkness, and it is perfectly possible to see clearly at 11 p.m. Conversely, in January it does not get light until 10 a.m., and is nearly dark again by 3 p.m. Further south these extremes are modified, but still influence dive planning throughout the year.

Sea temperatures are such that good thermal protection is required throughout the year. At its warmest, in the southwest, the sea temperature rarely exceeds 14°C, while in the North Sea 11°C is nearer the norm. Temperatures as low as 2°C are experienced in the North Sea in winter.

The water, when clear, is never the deep blue experienced in the Mediterranean or similar parts of the world, but retains a distinct greenness due to rotting vegetation, mainly in the form of seaweed. The British diving scenery is noted for its prolific plant growth and variety of flora and fauna. Blooms of plankton often reduce visibility during the summer months.

With all these variables it is not surprising that British diving is full of contrast. Very few world locations give such variety within a relatively small area, although there is a vast area of coast to choose from.

Visibility varies throughout the year and is dependent on weather, tides, plankton, geological conditions and industrial pollution. The region has some of the most unspoilt and natural coastal scenery in parts of the islands lying off the west Scottish coast, but some of the worst polluted beaches in Europe, mainly with domestic sewage, in the more popular holiday resorts. The North Sea has been used as a rubbish dump since the Industrial Revolution with both colliery spoil and other toxic chemicals being deposited in the coastal areas. The demise of the coal mining industry in the northeast of England has improved matters, but the discharge of chemical waste, raw sewage and other poisons affects both visibility and underwater ecology. Lack of efficient tidal discharge accentuates the problem in the North Sea. Its generally shallow nature in the southern section, and the fact that we share it with our European neighbours, all contribute to the problem in terms of diving conditions. Unpolluted rivers are often stained brown with peat if they run through a mountainous area before reaching the sea.

Where are the most reliable diving areas?

The Irish coast in general has some marvellously clear water with visibility in excess of 20 metres horizontally, and very little in the way of pollution, especially on the west coast. It does, however, bear the brunt of any Atlantic storms, and the west coast is often hammered by rollers caused by storms far out into the ocean. All the bad weather systems of the British Isles, in the form of depressions, move from west to east with the most common (prevailing) wind direction being southwest. The western-facing coasts are therefore very susceptible to rough water caused by strong westerly winds. Many divers claim the northwest coast of Scotland, with hundreds of islands, some large and inhabited, some no more than a bare rock outcrop, has the finest diving areas in the British Isles. Clear water, white beaches, the variety of underwater flora and fauna, and the sheer remoteness of many parts are all justification for this description. Because there are so many islands, shelter can always be found. Tidal streams are minimal over vast areas to allow relative freedom when planning diving.

The east coast of Scotland has been scarcely touched because of its remoteness and exposure to foul weather from the east. The Caithness coast of Scotland has some of the world's most magnificent sandy beaches with rarely a soul on them. Hundreds of shipwrecks lie waiting to be discovered off the east coast of Scotland and northern England. The eastern side of the British Isles tends to have much greater expanses of coast without natural shelter, and harbours are few and far between. This is an important consideration when going to sea with such a fickle climate. In spite of what is outlined above, much of the North Sea has excellent visibility until one reaches the populated areas further south. Here the sandy nature of the submarine geology plays havoc with visibility, especially in winter, and makes most of the inshore waters unfit for diving between November and May south of the River Tyne in Northumberland. Further north, excellent visibility is experienced in settled conditions throughout the year. The North Sea also boasts of hundreds of shipwrecks, and many war relics, most of them yet to be explored or discovered.

The southern coast of England skirting the English Channel improves as one goes west. The Kent and Sussex coast is subject to strong tidal flows and is an area of particular interest to wreck divers due to the heavy shipping traffic which has been a feature since Roman times. Moving west one reaches the most popular diving area of Dorset, Devon and Cornwall. Here the volcanic rocks, unpolluted water, numerous shipwrecks and generally kinder weather bring divers from all over the country. The southwest coast has many excellent harbours and launching spots for boats, together with a wide range of facilities for divers. Because of this area's popularity, those organizing dives during peak summer periods should investigate the expected diving activity at a site in order to avoid congestion.

Figure 10 North Wales, a popular destination for divers – Aberdaron

Figure 9 Scotland offers some of the finest diving – Scapa Flow

Figure 11 The South West has a great number of wrecks – Plymouth

Diving Conditions – The World

The variety of climate, terrain, population density and political stability throughout the world ensures that there is a vast range of diving conditions.

All diving conditions are affected by the common denominators of weather, mainly wind direction and strength, the presence or lack of tidal streams, urban and industrial areas with connected pollution effects, and geological influences.

There are many parts of the world which share the vagaries of weather endured by northern Europe. Conversely, many areas share a completely predictable warm, settled climate which produces ideal diving conditions for nearly the whole year. Very few places, however, are without sudden upsets in an otherwise settled routine of weather or sea state, and conditions can never be guaranteed.

As mentioned above, the wind is probably the greatest influence in terms of diving conditions. Any location exposed to the passage of wind over a large stretch of ocean is likely to produce a very rough sea state inshore. The large 'fetch' of the subsequent waves reflects storm activity far out to sea, regardless of local coastal weather conditions. Figure 12 shows the world system of trade winds, which were originally used in the days of sail to plot voyages round the globe taking advantage of their reliability. In southerly high latitudes the famous 'Roaring Forties' give an indication as to their fury and strength. Any coastline battered by the trade winds can be regarded as having unreliable diving conditions. Seasonal winds, such as the monsoon of Southeast Asia, blow in opposite directions depending on the time of the year. The summer monsoon, which brings rain to large parts of India and neighbouring countries, blows warm air laden with moisture off the Indian Ocean during the northern hemisphere's summer. The winter monsoon in the same region blows from the land, pulling down bitterly cold air from the Himalayas. Diving in such areas will obviously be affected, depending on the season of the year.

Many parts of the northern hemisphere, notably the Caribbean and the western Pacific in tropical latitudes, have some excellent diving conditions, but are subject to violent tropical storms in the summer months. The hurricane of the Caribbean and the typhoon of the South China Sea are the same phenomenon. Intense atmospheric energy is created within air influenced by warm seas and hot sun to create fast-moving destructive storms where winds reach 200 kilometres per hour with frequent loss of life and wholesale destruction of towns and villages. Many of the fine historic shipwrecks in the Caribbean were caused by hurricanes intercepting the Spanish and Portuguese treasure ships as they made their way towards Europe, groaning under the weight of gold, silver and precious stones. The recent discovery of Chinese porcelain in the *Nan-King* treasure ship in the South China Sea is testimony to a similar influence by typhoons.

Fortunately, modern hurricanes and typhoons are easily trackable by satellite and adequate warnings are given. Nevertheless, their course is highly unpredictable, and many cases on record show that ships in some areas which have 'battened down the hatches' escape, while others, who thought they were in the clear, capture the full strength of the storm.

Some parts of the world, notably the Far East, suffer from the occasional tsunami, sometimes incorrectly called a tidal wave. Walls of water up to 15 metres in height can cause widespread destruction of coastal villages when they strike without warning. They are produced by submarine earthquakes and generated by displacement of the seabed, and have nothing to do with tides. One needs little imagination to picture being caught up in a tsunami close inshore in a dive boat. It is in shallow inshore zones where their damage is greatest. At sea they are relatively harmless.

It is fairly easy to identify the popular diving areas of the world and to understand how they acquired their reputation.

The Mediterranean in general is blessed with clear water and very small tidal movement, its only link with the main oceans of the world being through the narrow Straits of Gibraltar. It is estimated that it takes water about 100 years to circulate around the Mediterranean. The months between April and October have long periods dominated by anticyclonic high-pressure weather areas bringing dry sunny conditions throughout. Exceptions to this are mainly in the form of thunderstorms, especially along the coasts of Spain and northern Italy, brought about by the influence of nearby mountains. Water temperatures in the Mediterranean vary quite dramatically over the year, dropping to about 13°C in February and climbing to 27°C in August and September. The eastern part of the Mediterranean in the vicinity of the Greek archipelago is the warmest, when summer air temperatures frequently exceed 35°C and 40°C is not uncommon. Pollution has been a cause for concern due to lack of tidal flow, especially in the Adriatic off the Italian coastline. Diving is best avoided near busy holiday resorts. Coastlines tend to be rocky and the diving is potentially good, but it has suffered badly from the effects of fishing. Large fish are rare, and many parts of the Mediterranean offer a limited range of marine life.

While the Mediterranean is generally calm, sudden storms are not infrequent, with short wave lengths, making it very uncomfortable at sea. Seasonal winds can be a problem, in particular the mistral, which howls down the Rhône valley and affects many parts of the Côte d'Azur. The sirocco is a very uncomfortable, hot southerly wind which blows from the Sahara Desert, bringing with it clouds of dust and making conditions very unpleasant. Malta in particular suffers from this wind.

Divers have for years been attracted by the coral reef areas of the world because of the beauty of the flora and fauna. Some of the most popular areas are the Caribbean, the Red Sea, Micronesia and the Great Barrier Reef in Australia.

Coral reefs in good condition are manna from heaven for underwater film-makers and photographers with their clear water and variety of life. In calm conditions the diving is excellent, but all these areas suffer from adverse weather conditions. The Red Sea is unbearably hot in the summer months, while the Florida Keys have to contend with their hurricane season. The Great Barrier Reef is affected by strong trade winds in places, and has the occasional tropical storm.

It is impossible to give a full description of every worthwhile diving area in the world. The west coast of Canada and the USA, islands in the Caribbean, islands in the Indian Ocean and the Philippines are all excellent diving areas with clear water and fine, calm weather as a general rule. Other parts of the world are yet to be truly discovered, but there are very few places where man has yet to venture under the water.

Figure 13 A Caribbean coral reef

Figure 12 World trade winds

Figure 14 The island of Gozo, a favourite with divers

Decompression

Decompression Tables

The object of a decompression table is to present the diver with a selection of dive profiles and ascent procedures which, if properly followed, should minimise the risk of decompression sickness. This is not a simple aim to achieve due to the many variables at work, especially where sport diving is concerned. Tables are based on mathematical hypotheses which in turn use various experimental test data, and are then used by military, commercial and sport divers. Experimental data is often obtained from very carefully controlled test dives performed using compression chambers, sometimes further validated by carefully controlled wet dives. In sport diving this degree of control of the dive profile is rarely achievable and in many cases not even desirable. This means the sport diver must understand the principles of decompression sickness avoidance as well as the mechanics of reading dives from a table. These same principles will also assist divers using decompression computers towards safer diving.

Table Terminology

Decompression tables present a selection of possible dives with a set of rules to enable this selection to encompass as wide a range of diving situations as possible. Sometimes, to enable a small and compact layout, only a few dives are shown. To broaden the applicability of such tables, rather complex rules or methodology are then needed (together with a degree in mathematics!). The BSAC '88 Tables employ the opposite approach, the rules and operational procedures are kept simple and straightforward, and the penalty of a multi-table layout accepted. In practice this should mean less chance of error in dive planning and conduct.

It is important to understand the correct interpretation of the various terms used in decompression tables. Some are fairly obvious, others may need explanation.

Depth
The deepest depth reached during the dive, measured in metres.

Ascent Check Depth
A depth reached on the ascent where a pause is made to verify the dive has been conducted according to the plan. A decision is then made on the remaining ascent procedure, either to continue to the surface or make appropriate in-water decompression stops. The *Ascent Check Depth* may be 9, 7, 6 or 5 metres, depending on the dive planned and the table used.

Descent Rate
The speed at which the diver descends from the surface to any deeper depth. The maximum descent rate allowed for is 30 metres per minute.

Ascent Rate
The speed at which the diver ascends through the water. The maximum permissible rate is 15 metres per minute,

up to the *Ascent Check Depth*. On all dives, one minute should be taken to ascend from 6 metres to the surface, and this 6 metres per minute speed is appropriate from deeper *Ascent Check Depths*.

Dive Time
The time elapsed from leaving the surface to reaching the *Ascent Check Depth* on the return to the surface. Not the total time immersed!

Ascent Time
A guideline time shown to assist in dive planning, being the minimum time to be allowed for ascent from the maximum depth of the dive to arrival at 6 metres. It is calculated at a rate of 15 metres per minute and rounded up to the nearest minute.

Surfacing Code
The code describing the diver's tissue saturation state on surfacing from a dive, a code using the letters A to G.

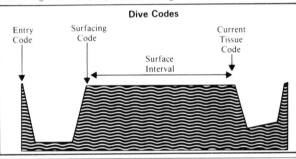

When a diver finishes a dive, the dive has a **SURFACING CODE**. During the course of the surface interval the diver's **CURRENT TISSUE CODE** changes. This is shown in the **SURFACE INTERVAL TABLE** for the appropriate **SURFACING CODE**. The diver's **CURRENT TISSUE CODE** at any time indicates the table which can now be used for diving.

Surface Interval
The time elapsed from leaving the water at the end of one dive to leaving the surface at the beginning of the following dive, or some other time interval following a dive when a current tissue saturation state is required.

Current Tissue Code
The code produced by applying a *Surface Interval* to the *Last Dive Code*. It indicates the diver's current tissue saturation state and the table on which the diver can now dive.

No-Stop Dive
A dive for which the table indicates no need for an in-water decompression stop or stops.

Decompression Stop
The time to be actually spent at the decompression stop depth indicated.

Decompression Stop Dive
A dive for which the table indicates the need for an in-water stop or stops to be carried out. Usually a dive with a *Surfacing Code* of G, although a few G code dives do not require an in-water stop.

Decompression Sickness Avoidance

Because of the wide variations in human physiology and the large number of factors that can affect your suscepti-bility to decompression sickness, no table can guarantee to protect you against all risk. On all dives your tissues will absorb gas due to the higher surrounding pressures, and this gas must later be released. Some of the gas will be re-leased during the ascent but on the majority of dives most of the excess gas is released on the surface after the dive. The quantity of gas absorbed and the manner and rate at which it is released are the main factors in influencing the onset of decompression sickness. Always remember that most of your time underwater is spent absorbing gas, with only a very short ascent time devoted to releasing suffi-cient gas to safely return to the surface. Your ascent rate is obviously an important feature of the dive!

Time and depth are crucial in deciding how much gas is taken up by the body; the maximum recommended depth for sport diving is 50 metres. As there is a faster rate of gas uptake on deeper dives, the time that can be spent underwater is severely curtailed, and eventually is so short that the dive is pointless for the risk involved. It is also important that deep dives are commenced with as low a gas tissue loading as possible. This means that in any series of dives, the deepest should be done first.

If a series of dives is being undertaken there is likely to be a build up of excess gas in the body tissues. This is because the post-dive gas elimination phase can be very lengthy. Depending on the dive performed, gas off-load-ing can take many hours, and lengthy repetitive diving can cause a potentially dangerous build-up of gas levels. For this reason it is recommended that no more than three dives be performed in any 24 hours and any dive series in-volving consecutive days diving to 30 metres (or greater) should be limited to four days, followed by a 24 hour break. As an example, on a week long expedition, this could mean halting diving at lunch time on the fourth day and starting again after lunch on the fifth day.

Bearing in mind that sport diving is a leisure activity, performed for enjoyment, it is always advisable to keep the risks within sensible bounds. The greater the gas absorption, the more complex the ascent procedure becomes. Very large tissue gas loads mean the diver can no longer ascend directly to the surface, but must 'stage' the ascent, stopping at various depths to wait for some of the excess gas to off-load. For sport diving it is recom-mended that dives carried out should not require more than 20 minutes total of such decompression stops in any 24 hour period.

As mentioned earlier, the rate of ascent is very import-ant and traditionally has been a weak skill amongst sport divers. Whilst the ascent is not usually the most interesting part of the dive, it is vital to your safety. Fortunately de-velopments in equipment and measuring devices are making ascent rate control simpler, but it is up to the in-dividual diver to make sure buoyancy is always under control, especially as the surface is approached. The maximum ascent rate from depth should be 15 metres per minute, until the Ascent Check Depth is reached. From 6 metres to the surface should take at least one minute, the maximum ascent rate being 6 metres per minute in this potentially hazardous ascent range.

The BSAC '88 tables have been designed to encourage slow ascents and incorporate the idea of maximum ascent rates, rather than fixed ascent rates. This means 'V' shaped dive profiles or other profile shapes such as a staged ascent up a reef face are easily planned and exe-cuted. Profiles involving a descent then an ascent fol-lowed by a re-descent, possibly repeatedly (a 'yo-yo' or 'sawtooth' profile) are not advisable. This is because each ascent can provoke bubble formation, which will then modify further gas uptake by the tissues in a way no table (or computer) can predict. It is also possible that bubbles formed in the venous blood, believed to be trapped normally by the lung capillary bed, may be compressed enough on the re-descent to break through to the arterial system and present a potential embolism problem.

Traditionally, decompression tables were con-structed by the navies of various nations and there-fore have their basis in military diving. As sport div-ers we are not prepared to accept the same incidence of bends as may be acceptable to those diving for military purposes. Usually the military diver has excellent surface support, in the form of recompression chambers, rapidly available to-gether with experienced and qualified attendants and medical personnel. Sport divers don't, and must therefore use a table which, as far as possible, avoids the risk of getting the bends. However, due to the differences in personal physiology, health, fit-ness and other factors, no decompression table can guarantee to remove this risk completely.

Following any dive or series of dives, the diver's tissues will be saturated with higher than normal gas levels for the duration of the surface decompression stop. These gas levels may mean that any further reduction in ambient pressure could provoke decompression sickness. Ambient pressure may be reduced by either ascending to altitude or by weather related air pressure changes, though the normal range and time scale of the latter mean they are unlikely to be a real problem to divers remaining at one level. If ascent to altitude is made by climbing hills or flying, even in a pressurised aircraft, then problems may occur if a safe surface decompression time has not elapsed. Detailed information may be obtained from the full edition of the BSAC '88 Tables, Levels 1 to 4, but generally ascents to altitude should not be made until a current tissue code of B is established. A current tissue code of A, normal saturation, is better still.

In addition, because of the rapid pressure drop experienced when an aircraft takes off and climbs to cruising altitude, such ascents are now believed to cause micro-bubbles to form frequently in the occupant's bloodstream. For a diver this is not only a possible risk after a dive, but also before a dive. If the flight is short, less than 90 minutes, there may be insufficient time for all the micro-bubbles to disappear before a dive is undertaken. Our advice is to use Table B for any dives made within 10 hours of landing, following short flights.

There are a number of physiological factors believed to increase the risk of decompression sickness. Some can be avoided by suitable abstention, such as reducing smoking and alcohol intake. Others, such as increasing age or excessive body fat, medical conditions affecting respiration or circulation, can mean extra precautions should be employed. The most significant precautions should be careful selection of suitable conservative dive plans, accurate dive profile monitoring and good control of safe ascent rates. Another useful precaution with the BSAC '88 Tables is to move to a more conservative Tissue Code. This gives a consistent method of increasing the safety margin without involving any calculations where errors can be made. A similar procedure can be adopted with the full set of all four air pressure bands, by choosing to dive on the next more conservative level set than the dive site air pressure would indicate – for example Level 2 instead of Level 1.

There is no doubt that many sport diving decompression sickness cases could be avoided if the advice in this section was followed – too many incidents feature deep or repetitive dives which are badly planned or executed.

Figure 17

TABLE B

SURFACE INTERVAL TABLE

LAST DIVE CODE	Minutes 15 30 60 90	Hours 2 3 4 6 10 12 14 15 16
B	B	A

DEPTH (metres)	ASCENT TIME (mins)	No-Stop Dives				Decompression Stop Dives							
3	(1)	—	∞										
6	(1)	—	80	504	∞								
9	1	—	27	113	148	188	255	272	284	292	300	307	314 321
12	1	—	14	52	67	84	116	129	137	143	148	152	156 160
15	1	—	8	31	40	48	69	79	86	90	94	98	101 105
18	1	—	21	27	32		47	55	61	64	68	71	74 76
DECOMPRESSION STOP (minutes) at **6 metres**							1	3	6	9	12	15	18 21
SURFACING CODE		*B*	**C**	**D**	**E**	**F**	*G*	**G**	**G**	**G**	**G**	**G**	**G** **G**

21	1	—	15	19	23	35	42	47	50	52	55	57
24	2	—	12	15	19	28	35	39	41	43	45	47
27	2	—	10	12	15	23	29	33	35	36	38	40
30	2	—	8	10	12	20	25	28	30	32	33	35
33	2	—	8	10	17	22	25	26	28	29	31	
36	2	—	7	8	15	20	22	24	25	26	28	
39	3	—	8	14	19	21	23	24	25	26		
DECOMPRESSION STOPS (minutes) at **9 metres**						1	1	1	1	2		
at **6 metres**					1	3	6	9	12	15	18	
SURFACING CODE		*B*	*C*	**D**	**E**	**F**	**G**	**G**	**G**	**G**	**G**	**G**

42	3	—	15	17	20	21	22	23	24
45	3	—	14	17	18	19	20	21	22
48	3	—	13	16	17	18	19	20	21
51	3	—	12	15	16	17	18	19	
DECOMPRESSION STOPS (minutes) at **9 metres**					1	1	1	2	2 3
at **6 metres**				2	3	6	9	12	15 18
SURFACING CODE		*B*	*C*	*D*	*E*	*F*	**G**	**G**	**G** **G** **G** **G** **G**

Figure 16

TABLE A

SURFACE INTERVAL TABLE

LAST DIVE CODE	Minutes 15 30 60 90	Hours 2 3 4 6 10 12 14 15 16
A		A

DEPTH (metres)	ASCENT TIME (mins)	No-Stop Dives					Decompression Stop Dives							
3	(1)	—	166	∞										
6	(1)	—	36	166	593	∞								
9	1	—	17	67	167	203	243	311	328	336	348	356	363	370 376
12	1	—	10	37	87	104	122	156	169	177	183	188	192	197 201
15	1	—	6	24	54	64	74	98	109	116	121	125	129	133 136
18	1	—	17	37	44	51	68	78	84	88	92	95	98	101
DECOMPRESSION STOP (minutes) at **6 metres**							1	3	6	9	12	15	18 21
SURFACING CODE		**B**	**C**	**D**	**E**	**F**	**G**	**G**	**G**	**G**	**G**	**G**	**G** **G**

21	1	—	13	28	32	37	51	59	65	68	72	75	77
24	2	—	11	22	26	30	41	49	53	56	59	62	64
27	2	—	8	18	21	24	34	41	45	47	50	52	55
30	2	—	7	15	17	20	29	35	39	41	43	45	47
33	2	—	13	15	17	25	30	34	36	38	40	42	
36	2	—	11	12	14	22	27	30	32	34	36	37	
39	3	—	10	12	13	20	25	29	30	32	33	35	
DECOMPRESSION STOPS (minutes) at **9 metres**						1	1	1	1	2			
at **6 metres**					1	3	6	9	12	15	18		
SURFACING CODE		*B*	*C*	**D**	**E**	**F**	**G**	**G**	**G**	**G**	**G**	**G**	**G**

42	3	—	9	10	12	21	23	26	28	29	31	32
45	3	—	8	9	10	19	22	24	26	27	28	30
48	3	—	8	9	18	21	23	24	25	26	28	
51	3	—	8	17	19	21	22	24	25	26		
DECOMPRESSION STOPS (minutes) at **9 metres**					1	1	1	2	2	3		
at **6 metres**				2	3	6	9	12	15	18		
SURFACING CODE		*B*	*C*	*D*	*E*	*F*	**G**	**G**	**G**	**G**	**G**	**G** **G**

Figure 18

TABLE C

SURFACE INTERVAL TABLE

LAST DIVE CODE	Minutes 15 30 60 90	Hours 2 3 4 6 10 12 14 15 16
C	C	B A

DEPTH (metres)	ASCENT TIME (mins)	No-Stop Dives			Decompression Stop Dives							
3	(1)	—	∞									
6	(1)	—	359	∞								
9	1	—	49	79	116	182	199	211	220	227	234	241 248
12	1	—	20	31	44	71	83	90	95	100	104	108 112
15	1	—	11	17	24	40	48	54	57	61	64	67 70
18	1	—	7	11	15	27	34	38	40	43	45	47 50
DECOMPRESSION STOP (minutes) at **6 metres**						1	3	6	9	12	15	18 21
SURFACING CODE		*B*	**C**	**D**	**E**	**F**	**G**	**G**	**G**	**G**	**G**	**G** **G**

21	1	—	7	10	20	26	29	31	33	35	37
24	2	—	8	16	22	25	26	28	29	31	
27	2	—	13	18	21	22	24	25	26		
30	2	—	11	16	18	19	20	22	23		
33	2	—	10	14	16	17	18	19	20		
36	2	—	8	12	14	15	16	17	18		
39	3	—	8	12	14	15	16	17	18		
DECOMPRESSION STOPS (minutes) at **9 metres**				1	1	1	1	2			
at **6 metres**			1	3	6	9	12	15	18		
SURFACING CODE		*B*	*C*	*D*	**E**	**F**	**G**	**G**	**G**	**G**	**G** **G**

42	3	—	10	•	13	14	15	16
45	3	—	9	•	12	•	14	• 15
48	3	—	8	•	12	•	13	14
51	3	—	8	10	11	12	•	13
DECOMPRESSION STOPS (minutes) at **9 metres**			1	1	1	2	2	3
at **6 metres**		2	3	6	9	12	15	18
SURFACING CODE		*B*	*C*	*D*	*E*	*F*	**G**	**G** **G** **G** **G** **G** **G**

Figure 19

TABLE D

SURFACE INTERVAL TABLE

LAST DIVE CODE D	Minutes 15 30 60 90			Hours 2 3 4 6 10 12 14 15 16	
D	D	C		B	A

DEPTH (metres)	ASCENT TIME (mins)	DIVE TIME (minutes) No-Stop Dives	Decompression Stop Dives
3	(1)	∞ 231 –	
6	(1)	– ∞	
9	1	– 8 29	81 96 107 115 122 129 136 143
12	1	– 8	26 33 38 42 45 48 51 54
15	1	–	14 19 23 25 27 28 30 32
18	1	–	9 14 16 18 19 20 22 23
21	1	–	6 10 13 14 15 16 17 18
24	2		– 9 11 12 13 14 15 16
27	2		– 8 10 11 • 12 13
30	2		– 7 9 • 10 11 • 12
33	2		– 8 • 9 • 10
36	2		– 7 8 • 9
39	3		– 8 • 9
DECOMPRESSION STOP (minutes) at 6 metres			1 3 6 9 12 15 18 21
SURFACING CODE		B C D E F	G G G G G G G G

42	3		– 8 • • 9
45	3		– 8 • • 9
48	3		– 8
DECOMPRESSION STOPS (minutes) at 9 metres			1 1 1 1
at 6 metres			9 12 15 18 21
SURFACING CODE		B C D E F	G G G G G G G

Figure 20

TABLE E

SURFACE INTERVAL TABLE

LAST DIVE CODE E	Minutes 15 30 60 90			Hours 2 3 4 6 10 12 14 15 16	
E	E	D	C	B	A

DEPTH (metres)	ASCENT TIME (mins)	DIVE TIME (minutes) No-Stop Dives	Decompression Stop Dives
3	(1)	∞ 271 8 –	
6	(1)	– ∞	
9	1	– 9	50 63 73 81 88 94 101 107
12	1	–	14 22 26 28 31 33 36 38
15	1	–	8 13 16 17 19 20 21 23
18	1	–	9 11 12 13 14 15 16
21	1	–	7 9 10 • 11 12 13
24	2⁻		– 7 8 9 10 • 11 12
27	2		– 7 8 • 9 • 10
30	2		– 7 • 8 • 9
33	2		– 7 • 8
36	2		– 7 .
DECOMPRESSION STOP (minutes) at 6 metres			1 3 6 9 12 15 18 21
SURFACING CODE		B C D E F	G G G G G G G G

Figure 21

TABLE G

SURFACE INTERVAL TABLE

LAST DIVE CODE G	Minutes 15 30 60 90			Hours 2 3 4 6 10 12 14 15 16	
G	G F	E	D	C	B	A

DEPTH (metres)	ASCENT TIME (mins)	DIVE TIME (minutes) No-Stop Dives	Decompression Stop Dives
3	(1)	∞ 332 45 19	7 –
6	(1)	∞ 484	81 –
9	1	–	9 12 16 19 23 27
12	1	–	6 7 8 10
15	1	–	6
DECOMPRESSION STOP (minutes) at 6 metres			– 6 9 12 15 18 21
SURFACING CODE		B C D E F	G G G G G G G

Figure 22

TABLE F

SURFACE INTERVAL TABLE

LAST DIVE CODE F	Minutes 15 30 60 90			Hours 2 3 4 6 10 12 14 15 16	
F	F E	D	C	B	A

DEPTH (metres)	ASCENT TIME (mins)	DIVE TIME (minutes) No-Stop Dives	Decompression Stop Dives
3	(1)	∞ 303 25 5	–
6	(1)	∞ 339	
9	1	–	23 33 40 46 52 57 63 69
12	1	–	6 11 14 16 18 20 22 24
15	1	–	7 9 10 11 12 13 14
18	1	–	6 7 8 9 10
21	1	–	6 • 7 8
24	2		– 7 • 8
27	2		– 7
DECOMPRESSION STOP (minutes) at 6 metres			1 3 6 9 12 15 18 21
SURFACING CODE		B C D E F	G G G G G G G G

Figure 23

SURFACE INTERVAL TABLE

LAST DIVE CODE	Minutes 15 30 60 90			Hours 2 3 4 6 10 12 14 15 16	
G	G F	E	D	C	B	A
F	F E	D	C	B	A
E	E	D	C	B	A
D	D	C	B	A
C	C	B	A
B	B	A
A	A

Using the Tables

Assuming a sea level dive site, with no pressure changes experienced during the last 16 hours, a Current Tissue Code of A can be adopted. This means Table A can be used for dive planning. On Table A, start by looking down the depth column for the depth equivalent to, or next greater than, the planned maximum depth of your dive. The column immediately to the right of the depth column is the ascent column. This gives the time required to ascend at 15 metres per minute to 6 metres, rounded up to the nearest minute.

The dive time section gives a range of times. Choose the time which is equal to, or next greater than, your planned dive time. All dives to the left of the no-stop line will not require any decompression stops during the ascent. Dives to the right of the line require stops as indicated on the decompression stops line, at 6 metres or at 9 and 6 metres. When you have selected your depth and dive time, look down the column to the surfacing code section and note the code indicated.

An Initial Dive

A sea level dive for divers on current tissue code A, to 20 metres. Using Table A, Level 1, look down the depth column until the 21 metre row is found – there is no 20 metre entry, so the next deeper depth is used. It is important that all table interpretations of this nature are made so that the safety margin is increased. The ascent column indicates a minimum of 1 minute should be allowed for ascent from 21 to 6 metres. A range of dive times are then offered, the first group requiring no in-water decompression stops, the second requiring stops varying from 1 minute at 6 metres to 2 minutes at 9 metres followed by 18 minutes at 6 metres. A dive time of 30 minutes is planned, this falls within the 32 minutes entry and will result in a surfacing code of E. If a rectangular dive profile is followed, with most of the dive at the maximum depth of 20 metres, then the ascent should be commenced after 29 minutes, to arrive at the 6 metre ascent check depth with the planned dive time.

On arrival at 6 metres, the actual dive time is checked against the dive plan and a decision made on the final part of the ascent. If the planned time and maximum depth have not been exceeded then the last 6 metres are ascended at the slower rate of 6 metres per minute. If either the time or depth have been exceeded then the rest of the ascent must be conducted according to appropriate contingency plans made before the dive. Note that in this case the chosen 30 minute dive time allows a 2 minute overrun margin in which the divers could still achieve a surfacing code of E and the maximum depth is 1 metre shallower than the table row used. Record carefully the surfacing code and time of all dives, especially if a series of dives are planned.

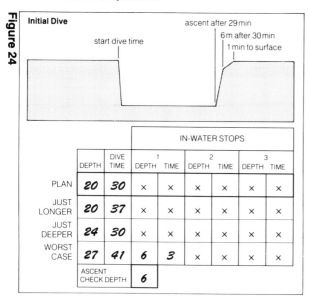

Figure 24

Planning a Second Dive

Enter the Level 1 Surface Interval Table from the left-hand column with the surfacing code of the last dive, from the previous example an E. The elapsed time since surfacing is then used to track the current tissue code, in this case 6 hours 15 minutes, which gives a code of B, being in the 4 to 14 hour band of the E row. This means that Table B should be used for a second dive at this time. The plan is for 18 metres maximum depth and Table B is used in the same manner as Table A was for the first example. The 18 metre row also indicates an ascent time of 1 minute and a dive time of 30 minutes is again chosen. Because the dive starts with a raised tissue gas load, the same dive time and a shallower maximum depth now result in a surfacing code of F, and are much closer to the no-stop border in the table. As the worst case scenario needs a decompression stop at 9 metres, this becomes the ascent check depth for the second dive.

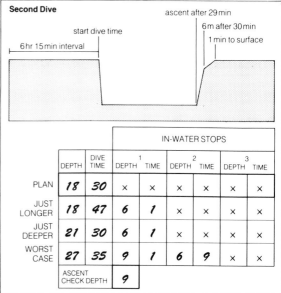

Figure 25

Subsequent Dives

The procedure is exactly the same as that used for the first and second dives. Remember the advice on series of repetitive dives which can cause a gradual build up of gas tissue levels. Keep to sensible levels of daily in-water decompression and take a break after a few days diving.

Altitude and Pressure Changes

A dive at altitude is effectively a dive starting from and finishing at a lower than standard atmospheric pressure. Whilst atmospheric pressure reduces with increasing altitude, it must be remembered that changing weather conditions also have a considerable effect on local air pressure.

Traditionally, decompression tables have been driven by the needs for solutions to sea level diving and have assumed standard atmospheric conditions. Some fairly arbitrary rule of thumb guidelines have been offered for those wishing to dive at altitude, and these have been based on height above sea level rather than actual air pressure.

A diver exposed to a lower than standard atmospheric pressure before diving will gradually adjust to that pressure, resulting in lower gas tissue saturation. If a sea level table is used, this lower tissue loading will be a slight benefit until tissue saturation levels are reached. However, it is the ascent phase of the dive (as always) which provides the problems. Here the diver must exit the water to a lower ambient pressure than that expected by the sea level table. This considerably increases the pressure differential experienced by the diver, promoting bubble growth.

It is clear therefore that standard atmosphere (sea level) tables are invalid for straightforward use when diving at altitude. Indeed, such tables can also be unsuitable for sea level diving under weather conditions that produce low atmospheric pressures.

The full set of the BSAC '88 Tables offers solutions covering atmospheric pressures ranging from standard atmospheric pressure down to 701 mb. These four sets of simply operated tables effectively cover diving from sea level up to 3000 m.

A decompression situation barely addressed in the past has been advice to divers experiencing changes in ambient pressure before, after or even between dives. This could be the result of journeys involving changes of altitude, either by surface or air transport, or weather changes causing fluctuations in ambient pressure. Advice covering these situations and mechanisms for subsequent diving is now provided.

Increased Pressure

Taking ambient pressure changes before diving first, there are two possibilities, the pressure change could be an increase or could be a decrease. If the air pressure experienced by the diver increases before the dive, as is often the case for a diver living at altitude and descending to the coast, the body tissues will be less saturated than the tables expect, giving a slight benefit as discussed previously. To cope with this situation the BSAC '88 Tables provide an Altitude/Atmospheric Pressure Chart and a Transfer Table.

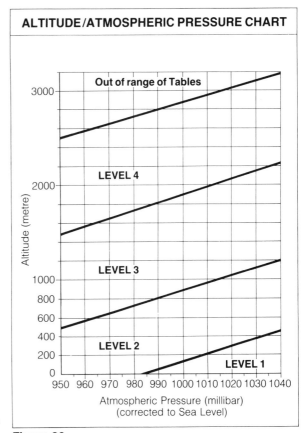

ALTITUDE/ATMOSPHERIC PRESSURE CHART

Figure 26

The Altitude/Atmospheric Pressure Chart indicates the Table Level to be used, using a known altitude and a current sea level atmospheric pressure, as provided in weather forecasts. (Weather forecasts give air pressures corrected to sea level.) By following the sea level atmospheric pressure vertically, and the known altitude horizontally, where these values meet the correct Level is shown. In borderline cases always choose the more conservative solution.

Pressurised aircraft are assumed to maintain a cabin pressure equivalent to LEVEL 4 which should be used to cover such flights. In practice, many flights are carried out with cabin pressures maintained at LEVEL 3, but assuming LEVEL 4 is an added safety factor.

The Transfer Table

This is used to relate the effects of changes in ambient pressure to the gas saturation levels of a diver's body tissues. Such changes can affect subsequent dives or even produce health threatening situations if they follow a dive.

TRANSFER TABLE					
LAST LEVEL CURRENT TISSUE CODE	LAST LEVEL	LEVEL 1	LEVEL 2	LEVEL 3	LEVEL 4
A	1	A	B	B	C
	2	A	A	B	C
	3	A	A	A	B
	4	A	A	A	A
B	1	B	C	D	D
	2	B	B	C	D
	3	B	B	B	C
	4	A	A	B	B
C	1	C	D	F	x
	2	C	C	D	G
	3	B	C	C	D
	4	B	B	C	C
D	1	D	G	x	x
	2	D	D	x	x
	3	C	D	D	x
	4	C	C	D	D
E	1	E	x	x	x
	2	D	E	x	x
	3	C	D	E	x
	4	C	C	D	E
F	1	F	x	x	x
	2	D	F	x	x
	3	D	D	F	x
	4	C	C	D	F
G	1	G	x	x	x
	2	E	G	x	x
	3	D	D	G	x
	4	C	D	D	G

Figure 27

The table is entered with the diver's Current Tissue Code, resulting from any previous dive and Surface Interval or stay at the lower ambient pressure. Moving across the table at the appropriate last level to the new level then indicates the diver's new Tissue Code, and thus which Table should be used for diving. If an x is shown then it is unsafe to change to that Level until further de-saturation has taken place at the current Level. This means the diver must stay at the current level until a valid current tissue code (A to G) is achieved. Should the dive be made some time after arriving at the new level, then the Surface Interval Table for that level will show any subsequent changes in tissue saturation and consequent changes in the required dive table.

Decreased pressure

Decreases in ambient pressure before the dive are more of a problem, in that the diver then has a higher than predicted tissue gas load, and will be off-loading that gas prior to the dive. Again, the Altitude/Atmospheric Pressure Chart will indicate the appropriate Levels to be considered, and the Transfer Table will give the new Tissue Code of the diver. If there is a delay before diving commences, the Surface Interval Table for the new level will again show any further changes in Tissue Code and therefore which Table should be used for the dive.

Flying before diving

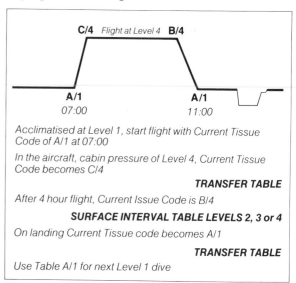

Acclimatised at Level 1, start flight with Current Tissue Code of A/1 at 07:00

In the aircraft, cabin pressure of Level 4, Current Tissue Code becomes C/4

TRANSFER TABLE

After 4 hour flight, Current Issue Code is B/4

SURFACE INTERVAL TABLE LEVELS 2, 3 or 4

On landing Current Tissue code becomes A/1

TRANSFER TABLE

Use Table A/1 for next Level 1 dive

Figure 28

A special case is that of flying to a dive site, even if the start and finish atmospheric pressures are within the same Table band. It is now believed that ascents to altitude, even in a pressurised aircraft, are sufficiently rapid so as to cause some micro-bubble formation and be a provocative decompression event. After a sufficiently long flight, these bubbles will disappear and the overall effect of the flight will be beneficial in lowering the tissue gas saturation as described earlier.

Short flights before diving

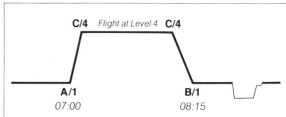

Acclimatised at Level 1, start flight with Current Tissue Code of A/1 at 07:00

In the aircraft, cabin pressure of Level 4, Current Tissue Code becomes C/4

TRANSFER TABLE

After 75 minute flight, Current Tissue Code is still C/4

SURFACE INTERVAL TABLE LEVELS 2, 3 or 4

On landing Current Tissue code becomes B/1

TRANSFER TABLE

Use Table B/1 for any Level 1 dive before 18:15

SURFACE INTERVAL TABLE LEVEL 1

Figure 29

However, short flights of 90 minutes or less must be considered provocative and the Transfer table can be used to cater for this effect. If a diver starts and finishes a flight at Level 1, but experiences Level 4 cabin pressure during the flight, the Transfer and Surface Interval Tables can be used to describe the process. Starting with a Tissue Code of A at Level 1, a transfer to Level 4 gives an equivalent Tissue Code of C. Using the Level 4 Surface Interval Table, Code C remains valid until 90 minutes have elapsed, so using the Transfer Table to return to Level 1 during that time gives a new Tissue Code of B. The Level 1 Surface Interval Table shows that the diver must wait until 10 hours have passed before Table A can be used.

Decreasing ambient pressure after diving

The question of exposure to lower pressure following a dive concerns most divers at some time. It typically occurs when a diver wishes to fly home following a diving holiday, but also occurs whenever excursions to altitude are made after diving. This includes trips made in surface transport, or even by foot! Even changing weather conditions can be considered, but generally the timescale they follow means they are unlikely to be a real problem on their own.

The period immediately following a dive, whilst the body tissues are still off-loading the excess gas from the dive, is effectively a decompression stop. If an excursion is made to a lower ambient pressure during this period, it can be the same as ascending above an in-water decompression depth before the stop is complete, and similar decompression sickness problems can result. It is essential that following a dive, no excursion to a lower atmospheric pressure is made until the gas tissue loadings are sufficiently reduced. For surface travel local atmospheric pressures to be encountered on a journey can be predicted, using the Altitude/Atmospheric Pressure Chart. The appropriate Surface Interval Table and the Transfer Table can then be used to indicate when particular stages of the journey may be carried out.

If the journey is to be made by air then similar predictions can be made, if in an unpressurised aircraft by similar use of Altitude/Atmospheric Pressure Chart, whilst pressurised aircraft can be assumed to maintain a cabin air pressure equivalent to Level 4. The Transfer Table shows that the earliest Level 1 Tissue Code permitting such a flight is Code B, and of course this assumption relies on the correct functioning of the aircraft in maintaining cabin pressure. There have been instances where malfunctions have caused loss of cabin pressure, when barotrauma is possible even in non-divers, so the risk to a diver with more highly loaded tissues may be accentuated. If this is a concern then delaying flying until Code A is reached is sensible.

For many years a variety of rather arbitrary advice has been offered. Now the BSAC '88 Tables describe this process more precisely than has been previously achieved and more informed decisions about the interval to leave between diving and making subsequent transitions in altitude can be made.

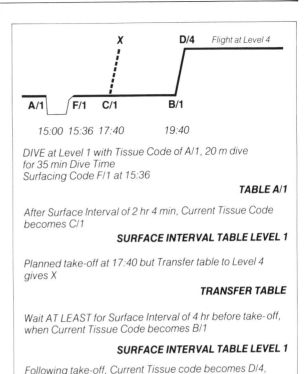

DIVE at Level 1 with Tissue Code of A/1, 20 m dive for 35 min Dive Time
Surfacing Code F/1 at 15:36

TABLE A/1

After Surface Interval of 2 hr 4 min, Current Tissue Code becomes C/1

SURFACE INTERVAL TABLE LEVEL 1

Planned take-off at 17:40 but Transfer table to Level 4 gives X

TRANSFER TABLE

Wait AT LEAST for Surface Interval of 4 hr before take-off, when Current Tissue Code becomes B/1

SURFACE INTERVAL TABLE LEVEL 1

Following take-off, Current Tissue code becomes D/4, at aircraft cabin pressure

TRANSFER TABLE

Figure 30

Precautionary In-water Decompression Stops

From the early days of sport diving there has been a belief held by many divers that a precautionary stop not required by the tables was beneficial. This practice posed no real difficulties in the days of one dive per day, but was more problematic when repeat diving became common. Traditionally tables with military or commercial backgrounds have been designed for rectangular dive profiles with strictly controlled ascent procedures, including a fixed ascent rate. Incorporating stops not required by the tables generally meant creating a dive profile not covered by the table, so it was frequently impossible to follow accurately the repeat dive procedure.

Precautionary stops

With the new concept of dive time instead of bottom time, slow ascents and extra or extended stops are usually simple to describe within the normal dive procedures of the BSAC '88 Tables. The 15 metre per minute ascent rate to 6 metres is a maximum not to be exceeded, rather than a precise target speed to be adhered to, and extra or extended stops can be included as part of the dive time. Thus divers who want extra security can easily make such ascents and stops within the tables and have no difficulty in planning and conducting repeat dives.

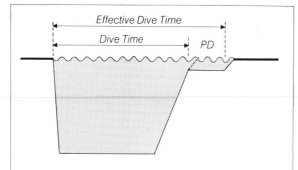

A dive is made followed by an ascent to 6 m at a maximum rate of 15 m/min

At the ascent check depth the Dive Time permits a direct 1 min ascent to the surface

A precautionary decompression stop (PD) is carried out before the final 1 min ascent is made to the surface

This extends the Dive Time by the length of the precautionary stop and may thus modify the diver's Surfacing Code

Figure 31

Long reef dives

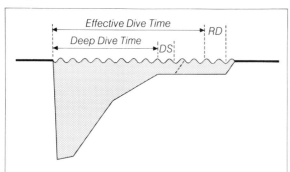

A typical reef dive is made followed by a decompression stop (DS), which could be either required or precautionary. At this point a normal ascent to the surface could be made.

Instead it is planned to prolong the stop at 6 m (frequently an interesting depth on a reef), which increases the effective Dive Time. At some stage this extended Dive Time will require a decompression stop (RD).

If the deep section of the dive required a stop then the whole of the 6 m portion may be required decompression.

Figure 32

Sawtooth Dive Profiles

Dive profiles where the divers descends, then ascends and subsequently re-descends are not recommended. This is principally because the ascent can produce micro-bubbles in the venous blood which will tend to accumulate in the lung capillaries. A descent in this situation could result in the increased pressure squeezing these bubbles sufficiently to allow them to pass through the lung capillary bed and so into the arterial circulation. The bubble then becomes a potential trigger for subsequent decompression sickness.

In practice some element of ascent and re-descent is often inevitable, but all steps must be taken to reduce the potential ill effects. Try and keep the variation to less than 6 metres, and to make any such event as near to the beginning of diving as possible, when the gas tissue loads are minimal. Re-descents towards the end of the dive with higher gas loads are likely to be more hazardous, as are variations when shallow where the relative pressure gradients are steeper.

If variations of more than 6 metres are made, it is wise to adopt penalising strategies, such as moving to the next most severe table. Thus if the dive had commenced as a Table A dive and a 6 metre sawtooth occurred, then the dive would be treated as a Table B dive, and an appropriate ascent procedure followed.

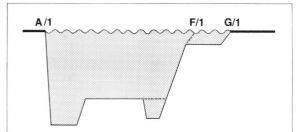

Normal ascending dive profile, A/1 to 27 m, 24 min Dive Time, results in no Stop and Surfacing Code F.

With re-descent of more than 6 m, Dive is conducted on Table B, 24 min Dive Time requires 3 min Stop at 6 m and gives Surfacing Code of G.

Figure 33

Diver separation which results in surfacing and then re-descending is an extreme example of a sawtooth profile. In this case any continuation of diving activity must be seen as a second dive, starting with the tissue code resulting from the first descent.

Decompression ambiguities

Remember in all cases of doubt when interpreting any decompression situation, the worst case should be assumed. Take the safer option, even if it means more decompression, above or below the surface. It is far better to curtail an interesting dive but be able to do another one than to suffer barotrauma and never dive again.

Decompression Practice

It has long been an axiom of good dive practice to plan your dive and dive your plan. Our current knowledge of the dangers of decompression sickness underlines the importance of that philosophy. The BSAC '88 Decompression Tables include a dive planning slate, together with a short summary table for emergency reference.

In planning a dive there are a number of parameters particularly important to decompression which should be noted:
1. Maximum planned depth – this has an obvious effect on the amount of gas that will be absorbed by the body tissues.
2. Planned dive time – this has an equally obvious effect on the final gas absorption levels of the tissues, gas which will need to be allowed for during the ascent phase of the dive.
3. Quantity of air needed for the dive, the amount allowing for the planned depth and time, with sufficient for an appropriate ascent, including any necessary or precautionary stops and a surface reserve.

When planning maximum depth and dive time, it is useful to record key elements of the dive profile and also some 'what if' solutions in case the original plan cannot be correctly adhered to. For example, it is well worth considering the possibility that the planned depth could be exceeded and noting an appropriate ascent procedure for that case. Similarly it is worth noting the correct ascent procedure should the dive time be accidentally overshot. Of course, neither of these situations should occur if the dive is properly controlled, but the best laid plans of mice and divers....

Besides catering for an overshoot on planned depth and dive time it is also useful to cater for a 'worst case' scenario. Plan a safe ascent from a bad depth and time overshoot – the limiting factor here is usually the amount of air carried.

The dive planning slate allows recording of the ascent information for these four situations: the intended dive, a further depth increment dive, a next time slot dive and a worst case dive. This means the diver can immediately

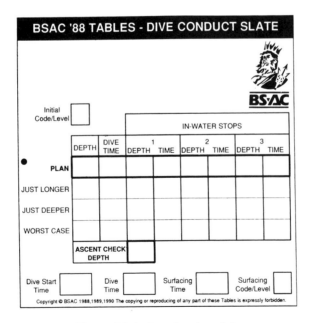

Figure 34 A dive planning slate

refer to either the planned dive or an escape route without the need to start replanning the dive underwater.

Dive planning underwater has never been a good idea and with modern flexible tables is even more undesirable, especially at depth. For the extreme dives requiring large amounts of in-water decompression any departure from the planned dive is not acceptable. If there is any risk that the plan might not work for any reason, the dive should not be carried out. Indeed, this is part of the reasoning behind the publication of a limited selection of dives on the reverse of the dive planning slate.

Besides the slots for the diver to insert dive planning information for a sequence of up to three dives, there are also diagrammatic time/depth profiles the diver can complete during the dive. This enables a simple record of the essential points on the dive profile to be kept, assisting both in dive logging and in planning subsequent dives.

On most dives, for the majority of the time spent underwater, the diver's body tissues are absorbing gas. The tissues must subsequently offload this gas when they return to normal atmospheric pressure. Most of this outgassing occurs whilst the diver is at the surface, with a small proportion being offloaded during the ascent.

This state of affairs can only be safely tolerated by the body if the absorbed tissue gas levels are not too high. For any particular dive a tissue gas load can be reached where a direct return to the surface becomes unsafe. The ascent from such a dive must then be performed so that sufficient offloading of gas takes place before the diver ascends through too great a pressure change.

Tissue out-gassing underwater can be allowed for by controlling the rate of ascent continuously or in stages. When decompression tables are being devised and tested it has been most convenient to follow the staged ascent procedure, with set 'stops' at certain depths being used, coupled with a steady ascent rate in between. This procedure is relatively simple to carry out in a pressure chamber and is applicable to water tests, especially when the diver has a surface controller.

Obviously, the sports diver in using such tables to avoid decompression sickness must follow the same procedures. If the ascent carried out by the sports diver varies from this set pattern, then effectively the table is not being followed and the diver is experimenting with a new table!

Actually measuring ascent rate has always been a difficult task for the 'free' diver. Traditional measures

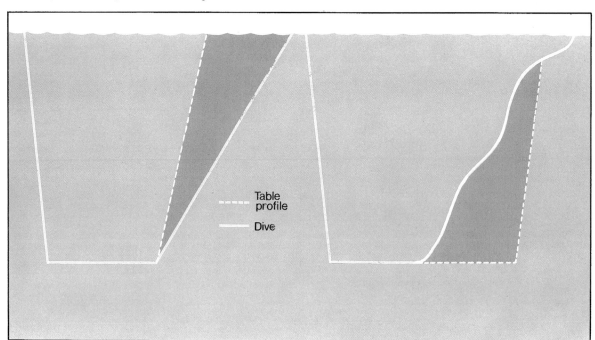

Table
profile

Dive

Figure 35 Older tables with 'Bottom Time' and fixed ascent rates mean if a slower ascent rate is followed the dive falls outside the target profile. This in turn means that the table has not been correctly used and can create difficulties for subsequent dives.

With the BSAC '88 Tables any ascent that does not exceed 15 m/min may be followed, aiming on arrival at 6 m for the planned dive time.

such as following small bubbles or staring fixedly at a watch and a depth gauge have all too frequently been found inaccurate. Some studies of ascent rates have found divers supposedly ascending at an 18 metres per minute rate actually averaging 36 metres per minute, with peak rates in excess of 50 metres per minute.

The advent of underwater instrumentation based on micro-electronics already gives us warning if predetermined ascent rates are exceeded. Hopefully even more sophisticated devices will soon be with us to indicate actual ascent rates.

Current thinking on ascent rates is that whilst the ideal would be a continuously variable and progressively slower rate, staged changes in ascent rate are practically more achievable. The principle is to reach shallower depths as soon as practicable, where gas will start being offloaded from most tissues. For this reason the BSAC '88 tables allow an ascent rate of up to 15 metres per minute until a depth of 6 metres is reached. As the rate of pressure change increases as the surface is neared, the maximum ascent rate is reduced to 6 metres per minute.

Obviously, slower rates of ascent are potentially good practice, provided proper measurement of dive time is made and appropriate decompression allowance followed. The old concept of 'bottom time' meant that if the inherently safe practice of a slow ascent was carried out, the diver would often be endangered by exceeding the profile envelope of the table. In producing a table of dive times to 6 metres, the BSAC is encouraging the practice of slow, safe ascents.

Users of dive computers often find that though the device calls for a short stop on commencing the ascent, as shallower depths are reached the requirement for a stop disappears. This is because the necessary outgassing has occurred during a slow ascent.

Practical techniques for measuring ascent rate when

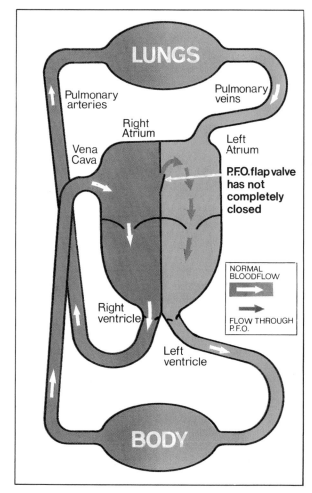

Figure 36

DECOMPRESSION SICKNESS SUSCEPTIBILITY

Physiological factors

* Pre-existing medical condition
* Fat
* Smoking
* Alcohol
* Fatigue
* Age
* Injury
* Dehydration
* Body temperature
* Medication
* Gender

'free' diving are few and the need for good initial training cannot be over-emphasized. Gaining an initial 'speed awareness' by performing carefully timed ascents from particular depths, with a visual reference such as a shotline, is important experience. Careful choice of depths will minimize the need for mathematics underwater.

A number of authorities on diving have long encouraged the practice of a 'safety' stop as a precaution on dives where the table allows a direct return to the surface. Making a 3-minute stop on such dives where maximum depths of 30 metres or more have been reached is often sensible and has the advantage of taking deliberate control of ascent rate at a crucial depth. Account should be taken of the increased dive time when arriving at an appropriate surfacing code for the dive.

Traditional tables have encouraged a blinkered thought process in considering dive planning, in the stark contrast they have shown to 'no-stop' and decompression stop dives. Many divers have believed there is some inherent protection by sticking to no-stop dives. Reality is not like that, the situation is many shades of grey rather than black and white. The fact is that a no-stop dive to the limit can be more DCS provocative than a dive just beyond the limit with an in-water stop.

Much of the reluctance to perform in-water stops has

been based on the difficulties of actually doing them in British waters. Many divers have now proved that with correct training and planning such stops are perfectly feasible. This should not be read as an encouragement to race to the hairier extremes of the table but rather to learn a technique which can make ascents safer.

There is no doubt that a direct ascent to the surface from many dives can encourage bubble formation. Current research is indicating this may be the cause of many DCS cases reported by divers following no-stop table profiles. The incidence of Patent Foramen Ovale (sub clinical hole in the heart) in the population could be as high as 25 per cent. It is currently impracticable to screen PFO cases with a diving medical and the ability of bubbles to shunt from the venous to the arterial blood provides a ready mechanism for DCS (see Figure 36).

Careful ascent procedures are therefore even more desirable. Many believe slow ascent procedures play an important role in reducing the rate of bubble formation as the body tissues out-gas. Although the decompression process is not complete, the surface is where the dive stops – when approaching a red traffic light it is better to be slowing down than accelerating! Awareness and control of ascent rate should be an important feature of every dive.

Whilst the underwater exposure in terms of depth and time are crucial factors in determining decompression requirements, there are a number of other factors which affect the risk of decompression sickness. Basically any factors which increase breathing rate or blood flow during the dive will increase the uptake of gas by the tissues, possibly to a degree the tables would not predict. Also any factor which decreases breathing rate or blood flow during the ascent will inhibit the offloading of the gas, again possibly taking the diver off the tables.

Many medical conditions can produce such factors, though most would be screened out in the diver's regular medical checks. However, these would not necessarily cover short-term changes which the individual diver must be responsible for detecting. Many drugs can affect the diver's respiration or circulation, with smoking being an obvious culprit.

Most divers are already aware of the increased risk of decompression sickness caused by an excess of fatty tissues, alcohol or tiredness. Dehydration caused by a reluctance of dry-suited divers to drink is also a concern, as is the change in blood flow caused by changes in body temperature.

It has long been believed that a resistance to decompression sickness can be obtained by gradually working up to depth and frequent diving. Whilst there appears to be some truth in this belief, the degree of work-up and depth exposure required is beyond the scope of normal sports diving. Certainly diving every weekend will not achieve any increase in tolerance, nor will the amount of diving performed during the week's diving expedition. Several weeks of constant diving are needed.

Indeed, divers on expeditions seem to build up a residual tissue gas level that makes them more prone as the week progresses and would be well advised to take a break from diving every few days. This is particularly important where deeper dives are being undertaken.

If more than one dive per day is being performed it is important that the deeper dive is done first, successive dives always being shallower. It is good practice to carry out only one dive requiring in-water decompression stops per day, though subsequent dives might benefit from precautionary stops.

Another practice which increases the possibility of decompression sickness is to repeatedly ascend and descend. It is best to attain the deepest depth of the dive early in the profile and from there always to ascend. With the BSAC '88 tables it is recommended that if a redescent of 6m or more is made, the dive should be conducted as

---

DECOMPRESSION SICKNESS SUSCEPTIBILITY

Physical factors

* Depth and time exposure
* Underwater activity
* Wrong dive sequence
* Multiple ascents
* Multiple dives
* Ascent speed
* Post-dive activities

---

though on the next more conservative table. In other words, a dive pair on Table 'A' having ascended from a maximum of 30 metres to 24 metres, subsequently returning to 30 metres, should continue the dive as though on Table 'B'. This is not a recommended dive planning procedure; the plan should always be to avoid the need to redescend.

The concept of adopting a more conservative table can be a useful ploy in other circumstances. Any diver concerned about the increased risk of DCS with age could adopt a policy of moving back one table more than indicated by their current tissue code. Other situations where the DCS risk is increased could be similarly treated.

The traditional method of coping with separated divers must be reconsidered. When the two regroup on the surface, an immediate redescent and continuation of the original dive plan is not possible. At the very least the redescent should be treated as a second dive, with an appropriate code resulting from the first immersion. In many cases it will be more sensible to abandon the dive. An appreciation of the increased DCS risk in this situation should encourage better dive techniques to avoid losing contact and incurring such penalties!

A better understanding of the problems caused by dives involving repeated ascents has impacted on the way in which rescue training is organized. For the deeper exercises the best advice is to halt the exercise at 6m and from there make a normal ascent, continuing the exercise when the surface is reached. For the shallower initial training in less than 6m, always plan to maximize the learning from each ascent and to minimize the number of ascents. Spread them over the training period and avoid mixing deeper dives with multiple ascent sessions; probably an important consideration for the instructor.

If it is necessary to perform a training ascent with a dive and the final ascent will not suffice, then do it early and avoid continuing the ascent above 6 metres. By performing the ascent at the beginning of the dive there is less chance of absorbed gas reaching a bubble phase on the ascent and thus causing problems on the redescent.

Where training programmes have a need for a number of ascents, plan to spread these over a range of appropriate experience dives. Should it ever come to the worst and a real rescue or emergency arises, then, of course, an important consideration must be to remove the casualty from danger. This means reaching the surface as soon as possible and normal safe ascent procedures will have to be compromised. Decisions here are based on the ability to treat DCS on the surface against the inability to treat drowning underwater.

Following the treatment theme, the value of rapid administration of 100 per cent oxygen to DCS cases is now well understood. As a first-aid measure it should be available, together with trained administrators, in all diving situations. The equipment needed to assist DCS casualties differs from that conventionally provided by emergency services.

Divers should ensure they have equipment to an appropriate specification and are trained in its use; contact the BSAC Coaching Scheme for details. The importance of this cannot be stressed enough.

Whilst it is important for divers to plan and control their dives it is also important that a record of all diving groups in the water at any time is kept by the dive marshal. This dive log sheet should record appropriate information whilst the dive is in progress and also give summary details of the dive when the divers are recovered. These details may then be used for planning later buddy pairs, for long-term records and, in the event of an accident, will form vital evidence.

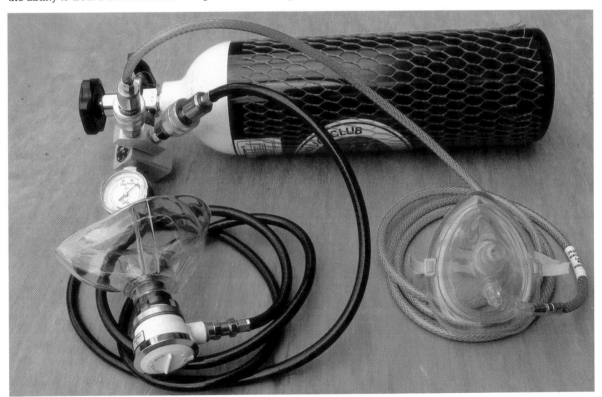

Figure 37 100% oxygen administration as a first aid measure

Dive Computers

A device that would automatically calculate levels of gas absorbed by a diver and then provide information that would allow a safe release of that gas has long been seen as desirable. Specifications for such a device existed in the early 1950s, but the first commercially successful attempt at such an instrument was the SOS Decompression Meter produced by SOS in Italy in 1959. This analogue device was based on a mechanical simulation of gas uptake and release by an 'average' body tissue. The simplicity of the model and its wide performance variation with temperature prevented most divers from accepting this solution. Later, various electrical analogue and digital devices were designed and produced, but none were commercially viable. This was generally because of difficulties with the pressure sensing transducer, lack of a suitable battery or the sheer cost of the device.

It was not until the early 1980s that suitable trans-

Figure 39 A selection of dive computers

Figure 38 S.O.S. decompression meter

ducers, cheap microprocessor and memory chips, suitable liquid crystal displays and appropriately sized battery units became available. In 1983 the Decobrain I and the Edge computers came on the market and the age of computer diving really commenced. These devices were improved and then a second generation of smaller devices such as the Suunto, Aladin and Skinny Dipper were produced at lower prices than the first-generation machines.

As more knowledge and experience in using dive computers became available, so designs have been further improved, later devices exhibiting extra features, improved displays and much longer battery life.

To actually sense tissue gas loads is not currently feasible. Analogue computers have used either a mechanical or electrical simulation of tissue gas uptake and release. The more successful digital computers have used either a table look-up or a computed value of tissue gas loading.

Table look-up means simply storing a traditional decompression table permanently within the computer's

memory and displaying the appropriate decompression requirements to the diver as the dive progresses. Whilst this would appear to have little advantage over the traditional watch, depth gauge and slate method it is in fact a significant step forward. The measurement of depth and time is much more accurate and the reliance upon the diver to take the appropriate readings and then correctly use them within the table is removed. It is important then to consider which table the computer is working to and whether it is suitable for the diver.

A further modification to simple table look-up is to perform a 'multi-level' table interpolation. This is by assuming that steps within the ruling rectangular envelope result in lower tissue gas loads and can thus produce an extension to the allowed dive time. It is obvious that decompression tables and ascents with staged decompression stops describe only a small section of possible dive profiles. Dive computers which compute various tissue gas loads as the dive progresses and continuously calculate decompression requirements from these values can more accurately simulate the state and needs of the diver. Such devices are often referred to as 'variable profile' or 'multi-level' computers. Using elapsed time and ambient pressure as inputs, calculations are repeatedly performed to update a set of simulated tissue gas loading values. From these values the most critical at any stage of the dive can be used to predict a decompression schedule.

The method followed to achieve these calculations is often referred to as an algorithm and it is the appropriateness of this algorithm which is important to the diver. Comparisons with conventional tables are only possible where rectangular dive profiles and the exact descent and ascent rates of that table are followed. Repetitive dive schedules are even more difficult to compare, because the computers are so precise in their measuring in an area, whereas tables suffer from gross rounding up

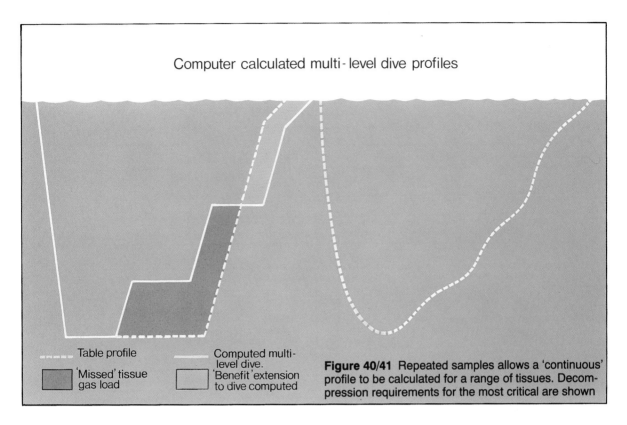

Computer calculated multi-level dive profiles

- - - - - Table profile   ———— Computed multi-level dive.

Legend: 'Missed' tissue gas load   'Benefit' extension to dive computed

Figure 40/41 Repeated samples allows a 'continuous' profile to be calculated for a range of tissues. Decompression requirements for the most critical are shown

on many sequences.

An essential part of all dive computers is an accurate clock. Coupling this with either a manual or an automatic switch means it can measure elapsed time during a dive and surface interval after the dive. Manual switches were common in early devices, often because of the short life of the batteries used. Problems all too frequently occurred when divers forgot to switch on before starting diving or inadvertently switched off their computers at the wrong time. Some models relied on a 'wet contact' system to start the computer running, but again problems arose when it failed to register atmospheric pressure before commencing a dive. Best are the devices that can be switched into dive mode simply by detecting a pressure change. Such an initiation is relatively diver proof!

The next essential element is a suitably accurate pressure transducer unaffected by temperature changes in typical diving environments. This can be used to provide the diver with both current and maximum attained depths.

Pressure readings, coupled with time measurement, are used by the computer to calculate other information for display to the diver. Remaining no-stop time, decompression stop time and depth, and total time required for the ascent are other desirable information displays. Some computers refer to the depth of the deepest

required decompression stop as the 'ceiling', above which the diver cannot ascend until the stop is complete. With improvements in algorithm processing speed pressure sampling rates have increased and better attempts are being made at ascent rate measurement. Currently only visual and audible warnings of exceeding set fixed rates are provided, though many divers would prefer an actual speed to be displayed.

Some computers have a second pressure transducer measuring air cylinder pressure and display that value. This can also be used by the algorithm, in conjunction with the clock, to calculate current air consumption and thus provide an estimated dive duration display. Currently, these devices are attached to the dive regulator via a high-pressure hose and make the computer not easily detachable and thus less portable. Ambient temperature is measured and displayed by a few computers.

Before the dive most computers will sense current atmospheric pressure, some displaying this directly, others using it as an altitude correction factor and displaying this symbolically. Many will also scroll through a number of predicted rectangular profile dives giving no-stop times against a range of depths. Other useful indications are a self-diagnostic test, often coupled with a check of all display elements and a battery state warning.

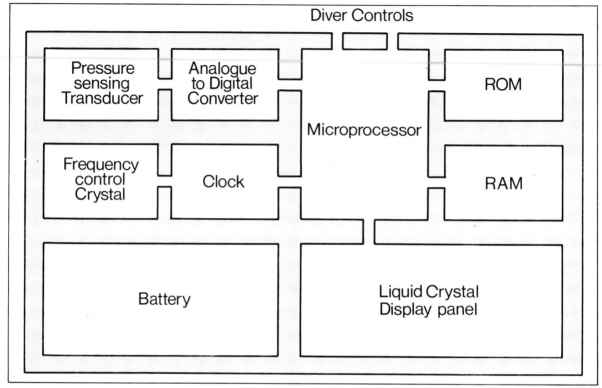

Figure 42 Basic layout of dive computer

Following the dive an important piece of information is the surface interval time, together with a predicted time to achieve normal tissue gas states. This is often backed up by advice on time before flying or ascending to altitude. Other displays include historical dive log information and look-ahead dive predictions, suitably modified by current tissue gas loadings.

All computers have limitations on their operating range, though they vary in their response to the user exceeding any of these parameters. The better ones provide suitable warnings and give 'best advice' to the user, whilst others give rather limited advice and information. They can also provide useful additional information for dive marshals, especially on ascent rate violations and detailed profile measurements.

It should be obvious that all dive computer users should read the instruction book and ensure they fully understand the operation and use of their device. Whilst the dive computer is the most accurate and reliable measuring instrument sports diving has so far enjoyed, never believe it is a substitute for properly planning a dive. At best it is providing good information on the gas uptake and release by a number of simulated tissues following your particular dive profile. It is not actually measuring your current tissue gas loadings, any more than conventional tables do.

It follows that exactly the same precautions to avoid decompression sickness must be taken. Remember, current computers do not account for the physical state of the wearer, or peculiarities within the dive profile or dive sequence. Make sure that you do not exceed the ascent rate specified by your computer algorithm, or you could invalidate its calculations. If the computer can be switched off, make sure you leave it on at least until it considers your being back at normal surface saturation. Many algorithms require up to 16 hours for this process, some as long as 18 hours. Should you suffer the unlikely event of a computer failure during a dive, your dive plan should give you an escape procedure. Abort the dive immediately and ascend to the deepest stop indicated in your bale-out plan, these stops being forecast from the worst case dive on the deepest planned depth of your dive.

A further consideration is how divers with and divers without computers can be mixed. The answer is they should not be. On most dives it is very difficult to really ensure that a non-computerized buddy will always stay shallower than a computer-wearing leader, or will follow exactly the same ascent profile. Switching from table diving to computer diving and vice versa is also problematic. The best advice in both these cases is to allow at least 24 hours' surface interval between such dives. Certainly do not allow less than the longest de-saturation time of the computer or table being switched to.

It is also worth emphasizing the desirability of keeping the diver and computer together before and after a dive, particularly if any changes in altitude or air pressure are to be experienced by either. The computer can only produce accurate forecasts of the diver's tissue states if it experiences the same atmospheric conditions, which includes flying in the cabin of pressurized aircraft.

Remember that the computer is a guide to help you avoid decompression sickness. You do not have to go to any limit it shows; staying inside those limits can only be better for your health. Please ensure you also read the sections on decompression practice and diving.

Summary Table of Dive Computer Features and Points to Note			
Pre-Dive	*Diving*	*Post-Dive*	*Other*
Function check	Current depth	Surface interval	Type
Battery state	Elapsed dive time	De-saturation time	Algorithm
Air pressure/altitude	No-stop time remaining	Fly/don't fly	Rect. profile values
Look ahead dives	Maximum depth	Log book values	Battery life
Cylinder pressure	Ascent time	Look ahead dives	Auto/manual on/off
	Stop depth/time		Readability
	Ascent rate		Wrist/console
	Air endurance		
	Temperature		

Decompression Diving

Decompression Diving

The first question to ask about any dive needing planned decompression stops rather than just precautionary stops is: why are you doing it? If a decompression stop MUST be made then it exists as a barrier between the diver and a safe ascent to the surface. The fact that it is not a physical barrier does not make it less dangerous, indeed it makes it more difficult to observe correctly. Just as with any other risk-increasing factor, decompression stop dives must be properly justified and all possible steps taken to minimize that risk. Only if the gains offered by the dive really do justify the increased risk should the dive be undertaken. Such depth/time exposures should not be done just for their own sake. Remember, there is usually more light and life in shallower depths, where warmer, longer dives may be carried out.

In assessing the suitability of a diver for a decompression stop dive, importance must be given to any factors which would increase that individual's susceptibility to decompression sickness. Some factors, such as increased tissue loading from previous dives, may be countered by delaying the dive or some other modification to the plan. Others, particularly physiological ones, may not be so easily resolved and may indicate that the person should not do such a dive.

Having recognized the increased risk of decompression stop dives, there are a number of steps which can be taken to minimize and control those risks. Careful dive planning regarding air consumption is certainly called for.

Besides the inability of the divers to return directly to the surface, another unusual feature of the dive is the requirement to stop at fixed, shallow depths on the ascent. The various skills needed in this technique should be learnt and practised on dives when such stops are not needed, in case the stops are not successful. Only when all the divers concerned have shown an ability to perform such stops comfortably should real decompression stops be attempted.

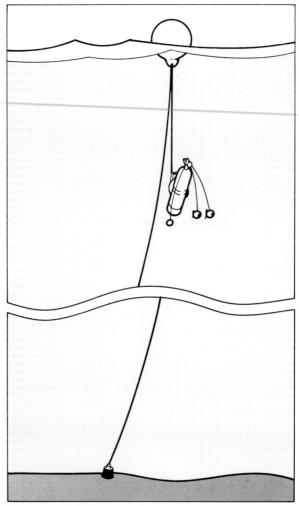

Figure 44 Cylinder securely attached, possibly with octopus regulator system at depth of shallowest stop

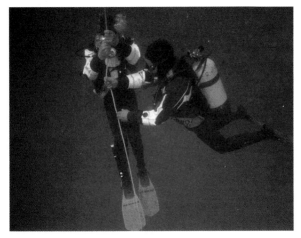

Figure 43 Divers at a decompression stop

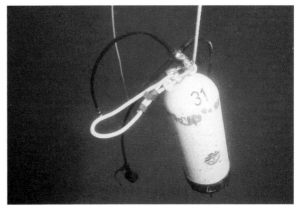

Figure 45 Single shotline with air supply

The first requirement is to be able to achieve neutral buoyancy at this stage of the dive. Bear in mind that a considerable amount of air will have been consumed during dives needing stops and that this will have an effect on the diver's buoyancy. Whilst the diver should be capable of neutral buoyancy at the stop depth, the most comfortable stops are often achieved with slightly negative buoyancy. This is when the divers have a shot line or similar to hold on to and it is emphasized that very little negative buoyancy is required. If the diver is having to work to maintain stop depth, either because of negative or positive buoyancy, the stop will be most uncomfortable and its accuracy may be compromised..

Do not forget that other factors may also influence a diver's buoyancy at this stage in the dive. Heavy tools or even the weightbelt may have been lost, giving positive buoyancy problems. Alternatively, weighty objects may have been recovered or a dry suit seal may have failed, making neutral buoyancy more difficult to achieve. Contingency plans must be made to cover these events.

The BSAC '88 tables deliberately have 6m as the shallowest stop depth. This is because relative pressure changes are less there than at 3 metres and wave action is also correspondingly less, making the stop easier to perform. Many computers give 3 metres as their final stop depth, but if the diver performs a stop at 6 metres the computer algorithm should be able to cope with that. Usually the need for a stop will clear in less than the predicted time for a 3 metres stop.

If decompression stops are to be made, then every effort must be made to make them as simple and easy as possible to perform. A substantial shot line with a trapeze bar is a very comfortable way of achieving this. The shot needs a weight (30 kilograms) or a secure underwater attachment system (anchor), plenty of surface buoyancy (50 kilograms) and consists of a rope of at least 15 millimetres diameter. When deployed it should be not too long, the idea being to provide the divers with the shortest route to and from the main point of interest of the dive. Marking the shot at the appropriate depth is sensible, if this can be accurately measured from the surface.

An emergency air supply should also be positioned at the stop depth, this often being on a separate line to facilitate both deployment and recovery. If two stop depths are involved the emergency air is usually positioned where it is most likely to be needed, at the shallower stop. However, in such cases it is safer to provide air at both stop depths.

Figure 46 To decompress comfortably in moving water, use a free floating shot which can be detached from the main shot on the ascent. The above system uses a crossbar at the shallowest stop depth, with an attached emergency cylinder. A reliable cover boat must be available to track the divers

Figure 47 Divers checking their dive computers at stop depth

An alternative system is to deploy a second free floating shot a short distance from the main shot, with a guide rope just below the deepest stop depth. This floating shot should have similar characteristics to the main shot but is usually only 1m longer than the deepest stop depth. Frequently this shot has the emergency air supply attached and has the advantage that if decompression is to be carried out in a current it can be detached from the main shot and be allowed to float free. Of course, this must be well planned in advance. All divers requiring the shot must be on it at the same time and a reliable cover boat must be available.

If the shot line is planned as the means of decompression then it is essential that the divers can guarantee to return to it. Otherwise some other plan must be made or the dive not carried out. When there is absolutely no concern over air supply a surface marker buoy of adequate buoyancy may also be used as a decompression marker. In this case reeling in the line slowly can help provide the correct slow ascent rate to the stop. However, once there, the line is less substantial and more difficult for a pair of divers to hang on to. Again the technique must be practised before it is used for real decompression stops. It is important that the divers will not be moved by either current or wind action on the buoy whilst the stop is being carried out and that a properly briefed reliable cover boat is available.

In similar conditions a procedure using 'delayed' marker buoys may be employed. Here a buoy, often a long sausage shape weighted at one end to project well above the surface, is inflated as the stop depth is reached. This acts as a marker buoy for the cover boat and the attached line is used by the decompressing divers. A variety of these devices abound, but one important consideration is the method of inflation and the amount of air required. Open-ended markers must be constantly under tension to keep the open end under water, but are easy to inflate from an octopus second stage or the buddies' exhaust bubbles. Closed buoys with mouth inflation tubes need a diver to remove the regulator, inflate the buoy, then replace and clear the regulator: not a recommended procedure. A further worry is that unless the closed buoy has a pressure relief valve it could be over-inflated at depth, so that it would burst on ascent.

Another difficulty is that upon inflation all these buoys give positive buoyancy to the diver holding them, which can be embarrassing if not dangerous. The buoy should therefore be of the smallest volume which can be effective. A neat though pricey solution is found in some buoys with a use-once-and-replace CO_2 cylinder for inflation, and also fitted with a pressure relief valve.

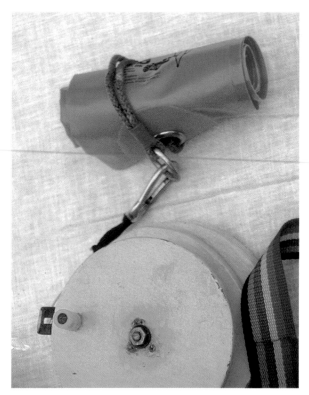

Figure 48 A 'delayed' surface marker buoy and reel

Figure 49 Marker buoy being inflated at stop depth

Figure 50 Inflating a marker buoy using a CO_2 cartridge

Figure 52 Nearing the surface the buoy requires constant tension

Figure 51 Fully inflated buoy heading for the surface

Figure 53 The buoy is clearly visible on the surface

The line used with these buoys is typically 10 metres long but only 3 millimetres diameter and gives similar problems to SMB line for the decompressing divers. Some method of storing and deploying the line must also be organised. With the open-ended buoys this can usually be achieved simply by stuffing the pre-attached line inside the buoy, leaving the free end with a small weight (500g) outside, before rolling up the buoy. This can be easily stored in a buoyancy compensator pocket until required. The closed type of buoy is often rolled up with the line wrapped around it, but this usually provides a potentially dangerous mess of loose line when the device is being deployed. A better solution is to use a mini SMB reel or spool, though this is more difficult to carry. All these buoys should be practised with and the

difficulties mentioned overcome before attempting to use them on decompression stop dives. Obviously, they need the same degree of planning and cover as any other 'free'-floating decompression system.

There is a particular style of diving that has long been practised when diving coral reefs, or similar sites where the area of interests extends from deep water almost to the surface. It is to start the dive deep and gradually ascend, the latter part of the dive being of long duration in shallow water and equating to a decompression stop. The problem is that no decompression tables have been produced to describe this shape of profile and if conventional rectangular profiles are used they are very punitive.

What divers following such profiles are attempting is to

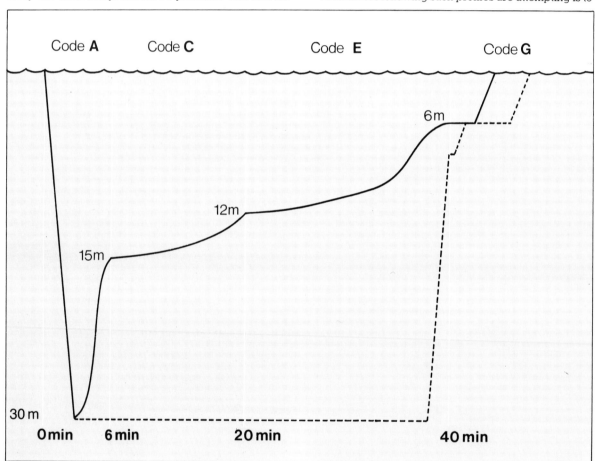

Figure 54 This multi-level dive starts with 30 m section on Code. A, which finishes on reaching 15 m after a 6 min Dive Time. The next section is then on Table C at a maximum depth of 15 m and has a Dive Time of 14 min, when 12 m is reached. Table E is then used for the third section of the dive, with a maximum of 12 m and 20 m Dive Time to 6 m, where a 3 min stop is needed before the final ascent to the surface. If the same dive had been performed under rectangular table rules stops at 9 m for 1 min and 6 m for 9 min would be needed.

match their gradual ascent to the decompression needs of their tissues, but in doing so they are, of course, writing and proving (or disproving!) a new decompression schedule. Whilst there may be merit in their logic, it is difficult to support such activities when the penalties for error are so severe.

Recently there have been new attempts to properly support such diving, in two ways. The first is the dive computer, which continuously monitors depth and calculates gas levels, thus supporting such a profile. The second is a technique to apply multi-level solutions to a decompression table. There is a way the BSAC '88 tables can be used to cater for an ascent in staged levels.

To use this technique the dive MUST be planned in advance and divided into a sequence of ascending stages, each being treated as a separate dive. From each

stage you are assumed to surface and gain the appropriate surfacing code, but, of course, you just ascend to the next stage depth. The dive time of the first stage is from leaving the surface up to arrival at the next stage depth, successive stage dive times being measured from arrival at that stage to arrival at the next.

Decompression requirements and appropriate surfacing codes for subsequent stages in the ascent are gained by using the table indicated from the previous stage 'surfacing code'. The final stage dive time must terminate at 6m, from where, following any appropriate decompression, a normal ascent to the surface is made. Whilst there is an implied safety margin in this, in that the ascents between each stage are imaginary, multi-level dives that can be conducted within a single rectangular profile envelope will give a greater safety margin.

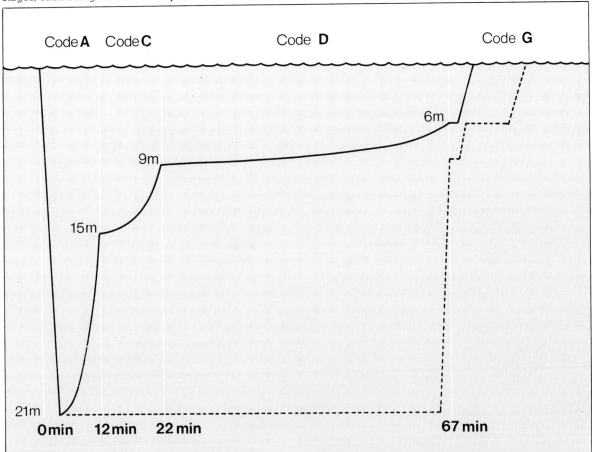

Figure 55 Another multi-level dive, split into three stages of 21 m/12 min 15 m/10 min and 9 m/45 min. The first stage is a Table A dive, producing a Surfacing Code of C, thus a second dive on Table C produces a Surfacing Code of D and the third stage gives a Surfacing Code of G, requiring a 6 m stop for 1 min. The enclosing rectangular dive on Table A requires stops at 9 m for 1 min and 6 m for 9 min. Note that this multi-level technique will not produce advantageous decompression profiles in all cases. Many such dives can be best catered for within a rectangular profile dive plan.

Wreck Diving

Wreck Research

Sooner or later the diver will want to learn more about the wreck he has been diving than is recorded in his log-book entry. Usually the wreck is one which his club and colleagues have been exploring for some time, possibly years, and they will probably know at least enough of the basic details to satisfy the inquisitive mind. Sometimes, however, these are not sufficient, or perhaps the wreck's name is not known. You may have been extremely fortunate to have discovered an unknown or uncharted wreck site. However, with today's electronic wizardry, this possibility is becoming a rarity.

Wreck research can be divided into three main categories:
1 Named wrecks. (Known.) Where the vessel has been positively identified by one means or another.
2 Un-named wrecks. (Unknown.) Where the vessel has not yet been positively identified and is known either by its latitude and longitude, or more commonly by a nickname.
3 New wrecks. (Unknown.) The site of an undiscovered vessel or one whose location is not known. Be wary, because a site not previously known and dived by yourself may be someone else's regular Sunday afternoon dive, however remote you may think it is!

Having defined the three categories it is plain to see that named wrecks are easier to trace and research than those which are unknown. However, the establishments and organizations approached for information more often than not overlap. With a known wreck, initial enquiries may be made to the Navy's Hydrographic Department or to Lloyd's. Copies of the Lloyd's shipping registers can be made available at reference libraries in most of the larger towns and cities, particularly those on or near the coast. An excellent source of reference is the *Dictionary of Disasters at Sea* by Charles Hocking. Unfortunately, the book is out of print, but again most reference libraries will stock it or order a copy for your perusal. As suggested by its title, the book is a dictionary listing in alphabetical order the names of many shipwrecks. Brief details are given, and where possible technical specifications, owners, builder, year built, year sunk and circumstances of loss. Perhaps the owners are still trading? Usually they are quite willing to access their archives and pass on information, which may include ships' plans, manifests and perhaps the odd photograph. The Guildhall Library houses many records of Merchant Shipping, including 'Lloyd's Loss Lists', whereas the Navy's historical branch is a better starting point for warships. The Hydrographic Department of the Navy and the Public Records Office are a contact for both merchant and naval vessels. The Public Records Office gives very little information out by mail, but you are invited to apply for a reader's ticket free of charge and look through their vast collections of records. Such things as a captain's statement of the sinking can be found and

for a moderate fee photocopied. Staff are always available to give you help in finding the relevant sections you are looking for.

More often than not the first two or three letters will reveal more sources if you so request, and gradually the story will unfold.

The un-named and unknown wrecks present more of a problem for obvious reasons. Initial enquiries should be directed to a local source. The nearest RNLI station may be able to help you, or the local newspaper, particularly if you have an idea of the date of sinking. Some of the older fishermen may recall a particular ship going down. Of course, the easiest way of finding out her name is to find the ship's bell or some similar object which may display her name or the shipping company. Ships' crockery on most passenger ships will at least bear the company's crest. A name plate from an anchor winch could help decide her nationality. You may even be lucky enough to find an engine maker's plate. Persevere and be patient. Was she a steamship? If so, how many boilers? Was she oil-fired? How many prop-shafts? Quite a large amount of information can be gathered by diving the wreck and making simple observations.

The following is a list of research sources where initial enquiries can be directed:

THE PUBLIC RECORDS OFFICE, KEW, SURREY TW9 4DU
A reader's ticket must be obtained beforehand if you intend to visit. As stated above the building is packed with information waiting to be tapped. Enquirers should ask for Information sheet No. 35, 'How To Use the Reading Rooms', and sheet No. 65, 'Records Relating to Shipwrecks'.

THE WRECK SECTION, HYDROGRAPHIC DEPARTMENT, MINISTRY OF DEFENCE, TAUNTON, SOMERSET
The current Head of the Department is Lieutenant Commander J.D. Pugh and enquiries should be addressed to him. The section maintains a computerized listing of all known and some unknown wrecks both naval and merchant in British waters. Accessing the computer may incur a minimal charge, depending on the work involved, but you will be informed beforehand. You may even be able to update the computer by passing on knowledge gained from diving a site, i.e., depth to sea bed, depth to highest point on wreck, is she in a dangerous condition? Should you be fortunate and eventually come up with a name for your wreck the department would appreciate you contacting them. It is not unknown for the department to reduce or even waive the cost of a computer readout for information passed on.

BOARD OF TRADE (WAR RISK INSURANCE OFFICE), PARLIAMENT SQUARE HOUSE, 34–36 PARLIAMENT STREET, LONDON SW1A 2ND

Figure 56 The famous clipper ship *Herzogin Cecile* wrecked at Starehole Bay, Devon, in 1936

The staff here may be able to help you with the details of Allied merchant shipping losses incurred during World War I and World War II. Details of the vessel's owners, and perhaps the ship's manifest may also be available.

LLOYD'S REGISTER OF SHIPPING, 71 FENCHURCH STREET, LONDON EC3M 4BS

The Information Officer receives a large number of written enquiries each month, so a quick reply should not be expected. However, brief details of the vessel together with details of her sinking are usually sent, especially if her name and date of loss are known.

THE INFORMATION SECTION LIBRARY at EMPEROR HOUSE, 35 VINE STREET, LONDON EC3

This is open to the general public between 09.15 hours and 16.30 hours weekdays, excluding public holidays for researchers to undertake their own searches. It is worth noting here that many ships worldwide were built under the guidance of Lloyd's surveyors, and so copies of ships' plans could be available.

TRINITY HOUSE LIGHTHOUSE SERVICE, TRINITY HOUSE, TOWER HILL, LONDON EC3N 4DH

The Information Officer can give details of dispersal, cargo, etc., provided the vessel's name and at least an approximate position are given. If the wreck needed a buoy above it to warn mariners of its existence, then Trinity House would have sanctioned the work. The wreck may have been dispersed at a later date and the buoy removed. Unfortunately, records prior to 1940 were destroyed by a fire.

THE SCIENCE MUSEUM, SOUTH KENSINGTON, LONDON SW7 2DD

The Department of Water Transport is an excellent source for details of ship construction and the machinery and equipment employed aboard.

THE NATIONAL MARITIME MUSEUM, GREENWICH, LONDON SE10 9NF

This is one of the few establishments which it is much better to write to initially than visit. There are many experts and calling in on the off-chance will almost certainly prove disappointing. Initial letters will be passed on by the 'Enquiry Services' to the appropriate expert. The Navigation Department houses a vast collection of charts which date back to the 1500s, whilst the library holds a very extensive and comprehensive collection of statistical books full of shipping information gleaned over the last two hundred years. The Manuscript Room contains hundreds of general layouts and detailed drawings of Admiralty vessels dating from the 1700s. If plans of your particular wreck are not available, do not despair – perhaps plans of a sister ship in the same or similar class are. Merchant shipping plans date from the end of the nineteenth century to the present day.

GUILDHALL LIBRARY, ALDERMANBURY, LONDON EC2P 2EJ

The library holds a vast collection of material from Lloyd's Corporation, and enquiries should be addressed to the Keeper of Public Records.

ROYAL NATIONAL LIFEBOAT INSTITUTE, WEST QUAY ROAD, POOLE, DORSET BH15 1HZ

The RNLI publish many books relating to shipwrecks and rescues in a particular area, and these may be purchased for a few pounds.

NAVAL HISTORY BRANCH, MINISTRY OF DEFENCE, EMPRESS STATE BUILDING, LONDON SW6 1TR

Another good source for information and details relating to Admiralty vessels, and should you or your club wish to make enquiries regarding the purchase of a Naval ship then write to: Director General of Defence Contracts (Naval), Section 85, Ensleigh, Bath, Avon.

WORLD SHIP SOCIETY, 35 WICKHAM WAY, HAYWARDS HEATH, WEST SUSSEX RH16 1UJ

For an annual subscription of £13, the wreck researcher can make enquiries for details of past and present shipping. Where possible the information is extensive and will include details such as the general specifications, builders, year built, later modifications if any, and an address for members to write to enquiring about photographs from a catalogue of some 60,000 negatives. Membership also includes a monthly copy of *Marine News*, and requests can be made through its columns.

Some of the above sources may be able to provide photographs of ships, but if not, will usually suggest a contact.

Finally the Salvage Association looks after the interests of ship owners and insurers who have lost something at sea. They also deal with genuine ocean salvors, but do not have the time or resources to deal with individual diving clubs. The Association should not be contacted by amateur divers, unless this is done officially through BSAC Headquarters.

Figure 57 The ship which taught the world about pollution – the 118,285 ton supertanker *Torrey Canyon* which struck the Seven Stones Reef, seven miles east of the Scilly Isles, on 18 March, 1967

Electronic Navigation

The ever-increasing influence on our lives of computers and electronics is nowhere more obvious than in the field of navigation and position fixing. Over the years, many divers and other small boat users have attended weekend or evening courses to try to learn the basics of navigation. They have been taught all about transit bearings, running fixes, compass fixes, etc., and have used various trigonometrical vector diagrams in order to work out the effects of wind and tide on a proposed journey at sea. Many others have spent time at sea using horizontal sextant angles, in conjunction with various geometrical techniques, in order to accurately determine their charted positions.

Almost overnight such techniques have been relegated to the category of old technology, alongside the lodestone and the astrolabe. Such is the impact of the microprocessor in the field of electronic navigation.

For a few hundred pounds divers can buy equipment which will not only give their current position at the touch of a button, but will store in 'memory' the location of favourite dive sites, will give a course to steer and distance off from each of these, will estimate speed and time to reach the destination, will give the helmsman an indication of any deviation from the chosen track through the water, and many more things.

The revolution mentioned above has been in the equipment; the technology behind electronic navigation has been around for some time.

The Decca Navigation system referred to was originally developed from the need for an accurate navigation system while undertaking night-time bombing raids during World War II. It was quickly realized that daytime bombing did nothing for the average life expectancy of the aircrews. Bombing at night when cities were blacked out was difficult, and the old adage of 'Necessity being the mother of invention' rang true again. Scientists developed a system of fixed directional radio 'beams'. Pilots flew along the beams, and a device in the aircraft told them if they deviated from their track. The beams were targeted on the cities to be bombed, and the system proved to be highly effective.

When peace was declared, the system of beams was modified into the world-famous Decca Navigation system, named after the company which developed and marketed it.

In principle, the system works by sending out fixed directional radio beams, each with a unique number/letter code. The world is divided into 'Decca' zones, the UK being included in the European zone. Each zone has its area divided into chains. There are twenty-five chains in Europe alone, and many more in the rest of the world. Each chain is served by a 'master' radio beacon and two or three 'slave' beacons, all on land, which are responsible for the geographical area within their chain. Beacons are positioned approximately 100 miles from each other. Each beacon is designated a colour, and so in any one chain there is a *red*, *purple* and *green* signal.

The concept behind position fixing using electronic means is quite familiar. Many of you will have used Ordnance Survey maps and will understand the system of grid references, or the use of co-ordinates, to accurately pinpoint locations on the map. Maps are covered by a system of grid squares, each grid line having a unique number. The location of any place is on the intersection of the grid lines, each place having its own unique map reference number.

The Decca Navigation system works in exactly the same way. To understand this it is necessary to study a Decca chart. (See Figure 58.) These are instantly recognizable by being covered in a matrix of position lines. Each chart has at least two different-coloured Decca lines which are numbered. On a small-scale chart the lines would form a pattern of curves. When seen on a large-scale chart, the matrix is seen to be more diamond-shaped than square. The important thing to remember is that the system of co-ordinates is exactly the same principle as that used on an Ordnance Survey map.

The old Decca Navigators were large box-like affairs, in the days before solid-state electronics and microprocessors. They were housed in the bridge of vessels that used them, and were only available under a rental agreement.

The modern navigator is no bigger than a small transistor radio, can be purchased for about £400 and can be easily mounted in a small diving boat with the availability of custom-made waterproof cases. It needs a suitable aerial, and usually a 12/24V power supply. It is literally a navigation computer, having either an LCD or LED display. In a larger vessel, with a dry wheelhouse, it is possible to link the machine to a printer which will give 'hard copy' printouts of the information required. In small boats, it is often necessary to protect the computer from the waves inside a purpose-built polycarbonate housing. Access to the controls is either through an opening window or a clear plastic cover. A recent addition to the market, however, is a completely water-resistant free-standing unit. At present this is only available with nine waypoints or 99 waypoints. No doubt greater memory will be added before long.

Divers who have used Decca understand how it opens up hitherto unaccessible dive sites. Many parts of the coasts around the world are low-lying, often mist enshrouded and are completely unsuitable for traditional position-fixing methods, such as transit bearings or horizontal sextant angles. Because of this they have never been fully explored, as it has been difficult, if not impossible, to maintain an accurate fix. This is no longer the case.

The machine shown in Figure 59 has tremendous potential for new dive-site exploration. It has the memory, for example, to store ninety-nine waypoints. A waypoint is a navigational term, and is defined as one of

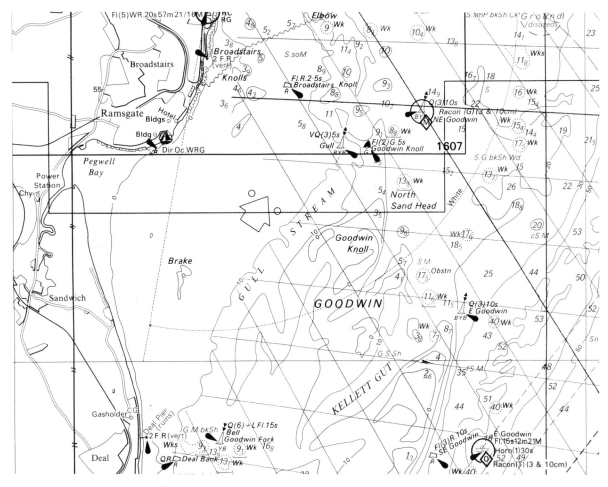

Figure 59 Navstar 2000

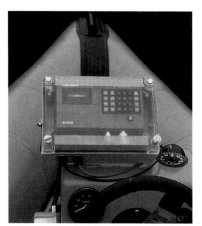

Figure 60 Housing for Navstar

the positions a vessel will pass through on the way to its final destination. A vessel planning a route along the coast may have to avoid headlands or areas of shallow ground and would therefore find it impossible to plot a straight-line course. A waypoint would thus appear at every place where the vessel made a major course change.

Divers, of course, use waypoints in a different fashion. Each waypoint can be the position of a dive site, either a wreck site or rock pinnacle, and once programmed into the computer will be held in memory until changed. Once the power supply is switched off there are internal rechargeable batteries, which keep the computer's memory intact and thus preserve all the data. With the facility to store so many dive sites as waypoints, it is necessary to have some sort of logic behind how they are plotted. It is prudent to reserve one waypoint for the place you want to return to. The others can be taken up by dive sites ascending in numbers either north to south, or south to north in the designated diving area. It is imperative that a separate record is kept of waypoints and the corresponding sites they refer to, just in case someone inadvertently wipes out the data in the machine.

The modern navigation computer is not difficult to use, and once one acquires the confidence of familiarity it is surprising how rapidly a degree of expertise is reached.

Once the machine's power supply is switched on it goes through a self-checking routine and tests the aerial or antenna connections/efficiency, signal strength, etc. A poor signal will seriously affect the accuracy of the computer. An initial position must be programmed into the machine, but there is an error margin of 3 nautical miles. As long as the position entered is no more than this distance, the computer will automatically adjust to the correct position. A word of warning here, however. It is vital that the vessel is not moved while the machine is switched off as there will be an obvious error when it is switched back on. This could occur, for example, when a small boat is moved along the coast by trailer in order to dive in a different location the following day. In this situation, it would be necessary to reprogramme the initial position of the new location before leaving for the dive site.

Waypoints can be programmed in and changed at any time. Accurate chart positions are programmed in as latitude and longitude positions *remembering to change the seconds to hundredths*. The Hydrographic Department of the Navy produce computer printouts of all wreck sites around the UK and for selected overseas areas, and these often contain either accurate latitude and longitude positions or Decca positions using the co-ordinate lines marked on the Decca chart.

Variables like magnetic variation and compass deviation can be programmed in so that the computer gives the helmsman a course to steer without the need for any adjustment. Waypoint alarms, either audible or with a flashing display, can be set to warn when the waypoint is being approached.

Another useful feature is the 'man overboard' facility.

Figure 61 A typical waypoint display

Designed with the yachtsman in mind who may lose a crew member overboard in rough seas, at the press of a button the vessel's current position is automatically recorded as a predetermined waypoint. This has exciting possibilities in a situation where the boat is looking for a site and the sounder suddenly peaks to reveal a large seabed anomaly. Pressing the 'man overboard' button stores the information and allows the boat to return with great accuracy to the site. Details can be recorded and changed to another waypoint, thus freeing the 'man overboard' slot for the next unexpected occurrence.

While following the display in order to reach the waypoint site is a common method of navigation, it is possible to navigate using the coloured Decca lanes on machines which have a dual-display facility. Switching to the 'lanes mode' it is important to remember that the gaps between them are divided into hundredths, so that positions of 36.50 GREEN and 57.25 PURPLE would place you midway between 36 and 37 green and a quarter of the distance between 57 and 58 purple. Once you have mastered this concept, you can find sites in much the same way as you would when using transit bearings. You drive the boat along one of the co-ordinates, and constantly monitor the other one, which will be either climbing or falling depending on your direction of approach. When the two readings match up with your predicted position, you need to mark the site for the detailed final search. This is an extremely effective method of dive-site location, but does require some practice and effective communication with the helmsman.

How accurate is the system? With a good aerial, strong signals and the right atmospheric conditions a degree of accuracy of ± 15 metres is achievable. Problems are encountered when these conditions do not apply, or at night when signals cannot be relied upon for their accuracy.

Problems can occur in the area where two separate Decca chains meet. Most machines have a choice of an automatic or manual logging on procedure for each Decca chain. Leaving the computer on automatic means that the machine will automatically log onto the strongest signal. Using manual allows the user to log onto the chain of his choice. Problems can be experienced in the boundary area between chains while in automatic mode. The computer can become confused by the two sets of signals and may give a course some 90 degrees away from where you really want to be. In this situation, the solution is to manually log onto the chain you are entering.

This section has been devoted to the Decca Navigation system, but it is worthwhile mentioning other successful methods of position fixing.

Over the years many boat skippers have used radar to accurately plot their position. Many radar sets allow the user to fix the position circles on the display on identifiable features, e.g., rocky headlands, and give the user an accurate 'distance off' reading. Using two or more such features gives an extremely accurate position fix, although a lot of practice is required before complete

Figure 62 Inflatable with Decca fitted

competence is acquired.

Satellite navigation systems are even more accurate than Decca, although the current cost is prohibitive to small boat users.

Personal Equipment

Wrecks are usually covered in a collection of sharp, pointed, jagged or abrasive objects with which the unwary diver is quite likely to come into contact. When the water temperature permits, the best screen against abrasion is given by a neoprene wet suit of reasonable thickness. This offers a degree of physical protection, but does not constitute an additional safety hazard if damaged. If a dry suit is worn, particularly a membrane type, then the use of a protective nylon or light plastic coverall will help. Holes can be cut in the coverall to provide access for suit controls and air supply. The wrists and ankles of the coverall should be elasticated or cinched to prevent them flapping about and snagging on wreckage, and also to reduce drag when swimming through the water. (See Figure 63.)

Figure 63 A coverall offers some protection against abrasions to a wet or dry suit

Every opportunity should be taken to produce a diver profile which is as streamlined as possible. To this end, all items of equipment should be examined and thought given to the position or modification which will reduce snagging to a minimum. For example, make sure there is no excess length of weightbelt strap dangling, trim aqualung harness straps, consider binding mask and fin buckles with electrical tape, remove that snorkel from the mask strap. It may be that the snorkel is not an appropriate piece of equipment for the dive, or that it is better stowed in a pocket or will be more streamlined if carried under a knife strap.

Combination consoles of contents gauge, depth gauge and compass can be at best a nuisance, and at worst a hazard, when swimming close to wreckage unless they are prevented from dangling free. The same applies to simple HP contents gauges. Most experienced wreck divers tuck these back into their waist strap or through the arm hole of waistcoat buoyancy compensators to keep them out of harm's way. Even such safety devices as octopus rigs can become a potential hazard in wreck exploration, unless proper thought is given to appropriate positioning and securing. A number of regulator first stages can be mounted in a variety of positions on the pillar valve. Try to choose a position which offers the least 'snag potential'. (See Figure 64.)

Figure 64 Arrange your regulator and pressure gauges to reduce snag resistance

A good sharp knife, surgical scissors or shears are an absolutely essential item as many wrecks are festooned with old nets, fishing line or rope. The traditional place for wearing a diving knife, on the outside of the calf, is not necessarily the best place, as it cannot always be reached when needed and may offer a greater chance of snagging. Many of the modern smaller knives can be worn easily on the arm or stored in the pocket of a buoyancy device. (See Figure 65.) Gloves are to be recommended, many wreck divers preferring medium-weight industrial gloves of canvas or nylon, as these are hardwearing, although not thermally efficient. (See Figure 66.) For serious work on wrecks heavyweight or even chain-mesh gloves are needed, as wet skin is soon insensitive to quite serious cuts, and razor-sharp edges can lie beneath the rust. Up-to-date anti-tetanus protection is advisable.

On most wreck dives a torch is recommended, and is usually essential if the wreck is to be penetrated in any way. It should be noted that not all the torches on the market are suitable for the wreck diving environment; what is needed is a high-intensity beam with a reasonable duration. There are many units on the market which fit the bill, although some regular wreck divers resort to custom-made units utilizing sealed-beam headlights, powered by rechargeable gel-type motorcycle batteries encapsulated in old pressure cookers, diving cylinders and the like. (See Figure 67.)

Strobe lights, waterproof electronic flashes which pulse about every thirty seconds, are becoming more popular aids to diver location. These may prove to be of significant use in wreck diving, especially in low visibility or as a means of easily relocating the shotline for the ascent. There would also seem to be some potential for using these strobes attached to the flagstaff of a surface marker buoy. An optical cover over the flash tube may be obtained in different colours in order to code different divers, uses, etc. (See Figure 68.)

Some divers find wearing protective headgear useful, especially when entering a wreck. A lightweight plastic canoeist's helmet will often suffice, although purpose-manufactured diving helmets with a built-in headlamp are available which have the advantage of keeping the hands free. If tools are to be carried on the dive then avoid the practice of stringing these on a weightbelt; they are best carried in a strong mesh goody bag which can be sealed closed at the mouth and easily jettisoned in a difficult situation. Avoid large-weave mesh as this tends to snag. Choose the close-weave 'shopping bag' style, with a relatively smooth finish which is still sufficiently porous to drain the water rapidly. Using a small lifting bag to carry tools is not advisable, as you will have nowhere to store them when it is needed. It may also leak due to wear.

Figure 65 Diver's knife mounted on the upper arm
Figure 66 Industrial gloves give some protection against sharp objects
Figure 67 Homemade lamp
Figure 68 Optical cover for strobe light

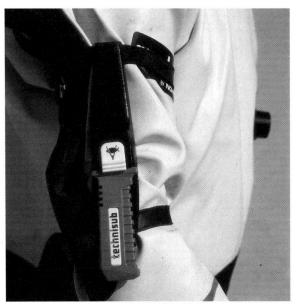

Figure 65

Figure 66

Figure 67

Figure 68

Surface Marker Buoys

In many diving situations it is extremely useful, if not essential, to have some means of indicating to the surface party the position of each diving group. If surface marker buoys are used to provide this function, then they can also serve as a means of diver recall. When wreck diving, however, use of an SMB may be impractical or even hazardous. Fortunately, when this is the case, the well-defined boundaries of most wreck sites mean that the diving groups are usually located within a small area. Furthermore, the site is usually well marked by means of a shotline, so the chance of losing divers is much less than on drift or general perambulating dives. When you are deciding whether or not to use SMBs, the nature of the site, the dive plan, and the number of other groups in the water should be considered.

When you look at the design of the SMB system study the purpose it has to fulfil, and the ease with which it can be used.

Floats

The float should be sufficiently large to stay easily on the surface, with a buoyancy of around 15 kilograms, and should also be large and bright enough to be seen from at least 200 metres. It must be immediately obvious that it is marking a group of divers and not easily confused with floats marking fishing nets or pots. Some SMBs achieve this by incorporating a pole with an 'A' flag attached. (See Figure 69.)

Lines

The line connecting the float to the reel must be strong enough for the purpose without creating undue drag when towed through the water. It will normally be about 2 millimetres in diameter, depending upon the material used. Braided line is least prone to kinking, though it should be remembered that all line 'comes to life' when immersed in water! Positively buoyant line will tend to float out of the way if too much is deployed, but it is always best to release the minimum. This will usually be a length equivalent to the depth plus 25 per cent.

Reels

A reel system will deploy and recover line easily when required. The most effective system is a simple hand reel with a ratchet. If the reel is made of a heavy material like steel or plastic, then the diver must maintain a taut line to the marker buoy if he is to avoid the reel snagging on the sea bed. By far the best material to use is wood, which gives the reel positive buoyancy. It can also float out of the way of the diver when not actively being used. In this mode it must remain connected to the diver, usually by means of a lanyard fastened to a strong point on the diver's harness or buoyancy compensator system. The lanyard should not exceed the length of the diver's arm, so that he can easily locate and reach the reel when necessary. It must also include a means of quick release should the diver need to rapidly detach the SMB system in an emergency situation. (See Figure 70.)

Figure 70 A lanyard clipped to the harness keeps the surface marker reel above the diver

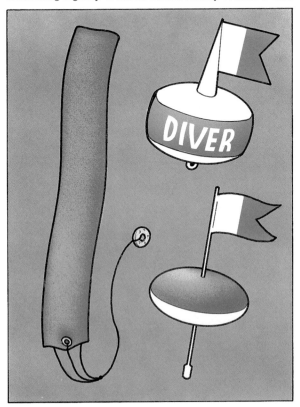

Figure 69 Three types of surface marker buoys

When descending, it is important that the divers avoid entanglement in the SMB line by holding it on the opposite side to their diving partner, and from potential snag points such as fins, knives and cylinders. Ideally, descending feet first will ensure the least chance of entanglement and the rate of deployment may be used as a guide to the rate of descent. It is also important that divers using an SMB avoid spiralling around a shotline, and indeed take every care to ensure the line does not become married to it. Normally only one SMB per group is used.

It is often in the ascent phase that SMBs create the most problems. This is usually because the divers ascend more rapidly than they can take in the line. As stated earlier, the reel must be capable of easily recovering the line, and it is important that the diver practises the technique until a good standard of proficiency is reached. Recovery of the line is normally a two-handed affair, so before the ascent is commenced all other equipment should be either stowed or handed to a companion. Keeping the line taut on the ascent should also ensure that the divers surface next to the SMB, which should be acting as a signal to protect them from redundant surface craft. Their own surface party should be watching that point, waiting for them to surface, and ready to move in and recover them. The quick-release mechanism on the lanyard may then be released and the SMB handed on to the surface party, or the next group of divers. Do make sure that the buoy and line are securely attached. Too many incidents have featured safety cover boats following drifting SMBs thinking they marked a group of their divers, only to find the buoy and line had become detached.

Figure 71 Divers using an SMB as a buddy line

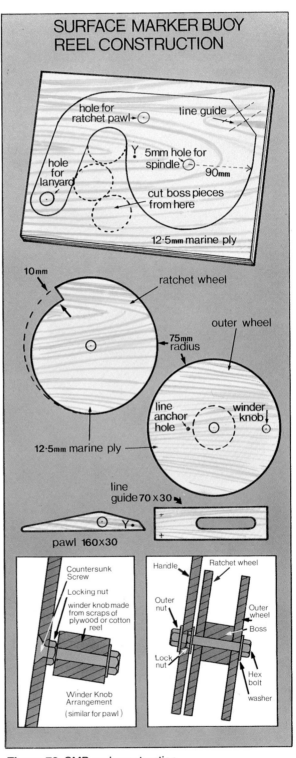

Figure 72 SMB reel construction

Shot Lines

Fixing a datum

When diving at any open-water site it is helpful to provide a fixed focus point for both the divers and the surface cover party. One means of providing this focus is by the use of a fixed line for the divers to descend. This line is marked by a conspicuous float at the surface, and is appropriately positioned for the divers underwater. Usually this situation is achieved by means of a shotline, and in wreck diving a grapnel-type anchor is often employed to fix the bottom of the line.

A grapnel which has been constructed with the tangs made from copper or mild steel rod is suitable, for if the anchor is found to be foul when it needs to be recovered, the line can be pulled until the ductile tangs are straightened out and the anchor comes free. Once back at the surface the tangs can be reshaped for further use. On most dives the top of the line is secured to a large buoy. However, this type of anchor will hold most reasonable-sized boats adequately in all but a strong wind or tide. If you are anchoring into a wreck, the first pair of divers down should check that the anchor is secure and has not fastened onto some part of the wreck-age in danger of collapse. (See Figure 73.)

Anchoring a small boat into the wreck is often seen as the simplest method of diving a wreck, but in fact offers many disadvantages. In order to safely anchor the boat, much more line than the diver needs has to be deployed, giving an unnecessarily long swim to and from the wreck. The boat will not be immediately available to pick up divers, or to protect the divers from other surface vessels – since not everyone respects the 'A' flag and it can take quite a while to start a motor and cast off even a quick-release anchor line. If only one dive boat is used, it should carefully patrol the dive site ready to offer immediate assistance to the divers. A further important point is the value placed by some divers and boatmen on the anchor itself. On far too many occasions the lives of divers have been placed at risk in attempts to free the anchor from the wreck following the dive.

If a weighted shot is used, it needs to be of adequate size (30 kilograms or thereabouts) to ensure that it cannot be dragged off the wreck by tide or wind action, or by divers pulling on the line when descending. Avoid leaving slack line in the water once the shot is deployed. This can be done by accurate depth measurement, usually from pre-dive planning, confirmed by an echo sounder when on site. Remember to allow for any tidal changes during the dive, but avoid the temptation to add a few metres more for luck. Adequate surface buoyancy is essential to support both the shot weight and the weight of the line if the occasional embarrassment and expense of lost shotlines is to be avoided. (See Figure 74.)

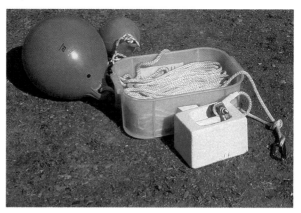

Figure 74 Shot weight, line and buoys

Figure 73 Anchor snagged on a wreck

Using a 'rope and pulley' system it is possible to construct a shotline that will always provide the shortest route to the wreck, regardless of the state of the tide. In most respects this is like a normal shotline, except that the line is not attached to the buoy. Instead, it passes through a metal ring which is attached to the buoy, and carries on back down to a second weight, usually of about 10 kilograms. It should be noted that this system must be carefully deployed and the weights and buoy equally carefully chosen if it is to be successful. (See Figure 75.)

Having deployed the shotline it is important to check, by transits or other position-fixing systems, that the shot is staying in position and not drifting or dragging with either wind or tide. Provided the surface buoy is of adequate size and buoyancy, this can also be used to suspend a marked decompression line with spare cylinders, if necessary.

If a wreck is being visited regularly, much time and effort can be saved if a shot can be left permanently marking the site. Care should be taken not to leave a hazard to other seafarers, and the sensitivities of people such as local fishermen should be considered. Often divers prefer to leave a shot that is so short that it only reaches the surface at low water slack. Another technique is to leave a strong shot firmly attached to the wreck but which is buoyed off at, say, 5 metres depth at low water slack. To the 5-metre buoy is attached a smaller line and marker buoy just reaching the surface at slack water. The smaller line and buoy are then thought

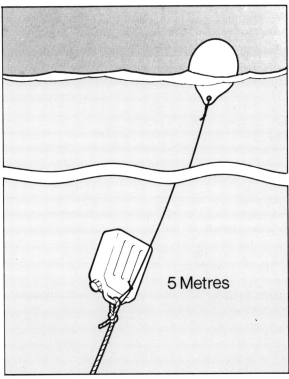

Figure 76 Sacrificial buoy

of as sacrificial in the event of bad weather or acquisitive visitors. Even if this marker buoy is lost, with good navigation and reasonable visibility, the larger 5-metre buoy can be relocated, grappled and remarked. (See Figure 76.)

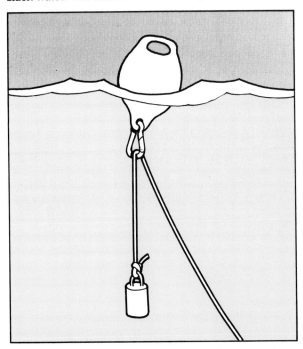

Figure 75 A lazy shot using the rope and pulley system

Figure 77 Shotline deployed underwater

When tidal 'slack-water windows' are short, the last diving group may want to carry out decompression stops in moving water. A good deal of careful pre-planning and preparation is essential to ensure this procedure can be carried out safely. One technique is for the group to ascend to decompression depth and then inflate a delayed SMB. This can consist of an air-tight cylindrical bag, sealed and weighted at one end, and attached to an appropriate length of line at the other. The diver inflates this underwater, and allows it to rise to the surface where it can be observed and followed by a safety cover boat. This technique usually requires that the divers carry sufficient air for the planned decompression. It is only suitable for experienced divers who are confident and capable of the buoyancy control needed to perform such mid-water stops. (See Figure 78.)

'Lazy shot'

Another technique is to use a 'lazy shot' that is attached to the main shot during the dive, but cast free by the last group on their ascent. This arrangement can be constructed more substantially, and have spare aqualungs fastened at appropriate depths for the decompression

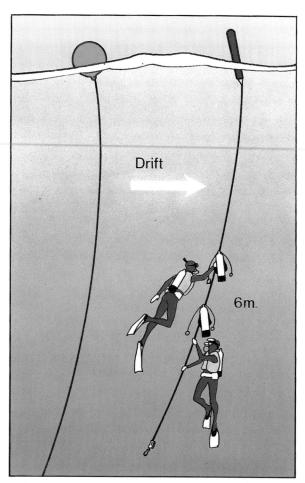

Figure 79 Divers drifting on lazy shot detached from main shotline

stops. (See Figure 79.)

Although it must be adequate, remember that the shot has to be hauled to the surface after the dive, usually by hand, so avoid using too heavy a weight. If the line is too thin, it will also be very painful on the hands when it is recovered. Wear work gloves to give a better grip and also to help protect the diver from the jellyfish stings which frequently adorn the line after a dive. Remember not to wipe them on your sweating brow! One simple way to assist in shot recovery is to attach a smallish folded lifting bag to the shot weight when it is deployed, which can be inflated by the last pair of divers before ascending. The bag should not raise the shot weight, but should provide sufficient buoyancy when fully inflated to make the job of lifting it by hand to the surface much easier.

'Wasters'

To avoid the problem of grapnel or shot removal at the end of a dive use a short length of sacrificial line ('waster') of low breaking strain to attach the shotline to the wreck. A 3-metre waster is attached to the weighted end of the

Figure 78 Delayed SMB

main shotline before the shot is deployed. The first pair of divers then attach the free end of the waster to a suitable part of the wreck, before freeing the weight or grapnel. To avoid the waster tangling during deployment, its free end may be tucked once into the lay of the main line. Divers may now continue without the worry of a shotline clearance task complicating the end of the dive, as the waster can easily be snapped and the already freed shot or grapnel recovered by the surface party after diving has finished. (See Figure 80.)

Mini-shot

One method which works well in good visibility is the use of a rapid deployment mini-shot. This consists of a cylindrical bobbin wound with an appropriate quantity of lightweight line with a 1 or 2 kilogram weight attached. An empty sealed plastic bottle wound with the right length of 1 to 3 millimetre line can replace more expensive polyurethane bobbins. When the boat arrives on the site the system is thrown overboard and, assuming the line remains untangled, the wreck is rapidly marked. The small size of the line ensures minimum resistance to the falling shot, whilst the low-profile float makes it less likely to be blown off site. Obviously, it is essential that divers avoid contact with the line to prevent it being pulled off the wreck. To give a more secure descent line, the first pair of divers can take with them a more substantial shotline and attach it to a suitable part of the wreck, possibly using the waster technique mentioned above. Recovery of the mini-shot is usually straightforward, although the first divers can cut the weight free and attach it to the main shotline, leaving the surface party to recover the float and the lightweight line. It is important that divers avoid becoming entangled with such lightweight shotlines. This system will not work successfully in conditions where visibility is less than 4 metres. (See Figure 81.)

BUOYED SHOT SECURED TO WRECK BY 'WASTER'. SHOT WEIGHT SUPPORTED BY SMALL LIFTING BAG.

waster line

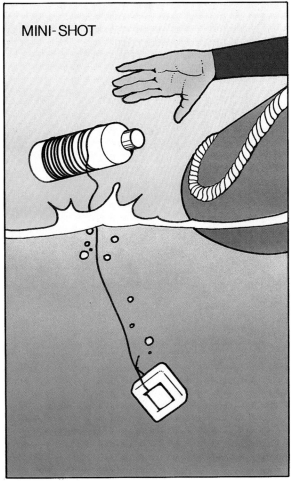

MINI-SHOT

Figure 80

Figure 81 Mini-shot

Bottom Lines

On many wreck dives the planned and safest way back to the surface is by ascending the shot- or anchor line. This demands that the diver is able to find his way back to the ascent line at the end of the dive. The orientation and navigational skills this requires may be beyond the diver's experience, especially in reduced visibility. To overcome these difficulties bottom lines are often used to trace a way back to the end of the shotline. The line is stored on a reel for simple deployment and has a carabiner on the end for easy underwater attachment to the shotline. It is recommended that any bottom line used should be of the non-floating variety, preferably braided, containing a lead core. Floating bottom lines are a distinct hazard, especially in the low visibility that causes them to be needed. (See Figure 82.)

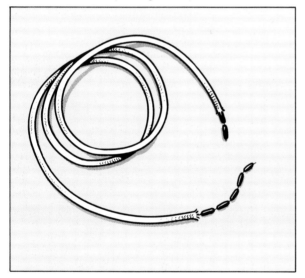

Figure 82 Lead-cored bottom line

Often the same reel for a surface marker buoy is used, but it is important that the different requirements of a bottom line system are understood. Firstly, there are those relating to a floating and non-floating line. Secondly, the reel itself could be a hazard if left above the diver. As it is in use deploying or recovering line whenever the diver is mobile and can normally be placed on the 'bottom' when the diver is stationary, it is better for the reel to be slightly negatively buoyant. This is usually the case when wound with leaded line, but if it is inherently positively buoyant this will become significant when most of the line is unreeled. Lastly, it is usually best if the reel is not attached to the diver, only hand-held, so that it is less likely to be a problem in an emergency situation.

Although much wreck diving is performed in separate groups, which compete rather than co-operate, there are advantages in the project team approach. Suitably marked fixed lines are placed on the site, which give divers assistance with both position and distance from

the shot. This is somewhat analogous to the concept of fixed ropes in mountaineering. Tags on the lines can indicate distance from the shot, and a simple letter code can differentiate between guide ropes leading to different features of the wreck. Different colours may be helpful, but if this is the only differentiating factor, confusion is possible in deeper, darker water, even when torches are used. (See Figure 83.)

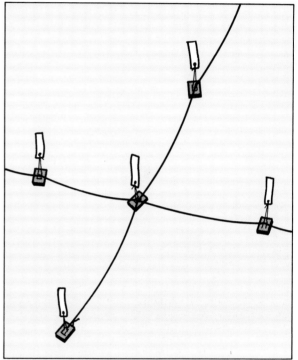

Figure 83 Weighted bottom line with tags

Whilst on the subject of lines, the use of the all-pervading 5-millimetre-diameter polypropylene rope used as cable duct draw-cord by telephone and electrical engineers is rarely appropriate in diving. Unfortunately, its wide availability means it is often employed in situations where it compromises diver safety. Woven or braided cords of an appropriate diameter and strength are much easier to handle and less prone to kinking.

No discussion of the use of line underwater would be complete without some mention of entanglement. Ropes, lines and nets underwater are a severe hazard to any diver and should be treated with maximum caution. Avoidance is obviously a sound policy. When this is not possible, as in the case of shotline, SMB line or bottom line use, keep the line as clear of potential snag points as possible. Deploy the line at arm's length, and avoid swimming over it. Any horizontal line is best laid on the bottom, and any other line is best at as close an angle to the vertical as possible. Ropes with a shallow angle to the vertical have featured in more than one incident where an octopus regulator, or some other piece of attached equipment, has snagged and interfered with an emergency ascent. It is helpful if all lines are as taut as practicable, as this will reduce the danger of snagging, and also help in freeing or cutting should entanglement occur.

One of the first accessories purchased by most divers is a diving knife, and once the visions of shark fights disappear, it is worn as a means of cutting the diver free of underwater entanglements. Unfortunately, the traditional-style diver's knife is not the most practical solution to many real entanglement situations. As most blades are of stainless steel, it is difficult to keep a really sharp cutting edge; a serrated or saw-tooth edge is more useful for cutting taut rope or cable underwater. For cutting nets or monofilament line, purpose-designed knives are available or small shears are very effective. The line is more easily cut when under some tension, which in many cases may be provided by the entangled diver becoming positively buoyant. (See Figure 85.)

Usual points of entrapment are the regulator first stage/ pillar valve and the fins/legs, areas which are difficult for the diver concerned to see or reach. This means that a buddy is the ideal person to effect the freeing, and the entangled diver should remain still and calm whilst this occurs.

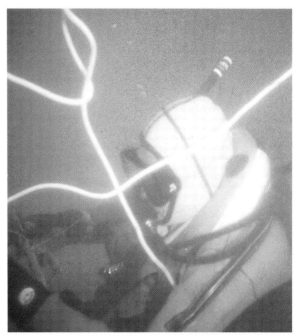

Figure 84 Diver entangled in line and net

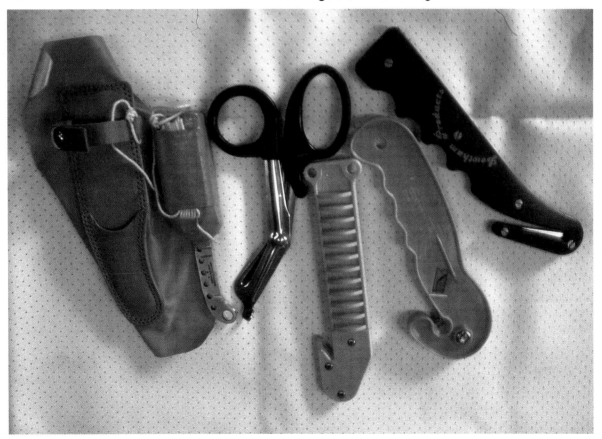

Figure 85 Specialist tools for line cutting

Wreck Detection

For the ardent wreck diver and researcher there is nothing more satisfying than finding and then diving on the wreck site which has been a target for your research, and may well have taken many hours of your time. Elsewhere in this manual is a comprehensive guide on how to research your wreck. This section is meant to be a background on modern methods of wreck detection, especially those involving the electronic equipment now readily available and within a price range that either individuals or diving clubs can afford.

Never before have we had so much technology to help us in our efforts to detect new wrecks. Contrast the search and detection methods today compared to twenty years ago, when teams of amateur divers were looking for the Spanish galleon wreck of the *Santa Maria de la Rosa* in Blasket Sound. Very accomplished swim-line search techniques were developed by the divers in an area with strong tidal streams. Incredibly, they covered some 15 million square metres of the sea bed before they found the site, near a previously uncharted rock pinnacle which they were convinced had ripped the bottom out of the vessel on the dangerous Stromboli Reef.

Very different techniques would be employed today using equipment in common use.

The combination of electronic navigation systems like the Decca Navigator and the use of proton magnetometers has revolutionized wreck detection, and made otherwise impossible projects possible.

In many parts of the world the traditional methods of position fixing, relying on vision on fixed objects, are rendered inoperable either because the site is too far out to sea or because of unreliable surface visibility. Electronic navigation systems, as described elsewhere in this book, give divers the opportunity to explore and dive, systematically, in areas where they were previously wasting their time. An example of this is the east coast of England, where depths, in places, do not exceed 30 metres up to 30 miles at sea. The area is littered with shipwrecks, many accurately charted after a fairly recent hydrological survey. Wreck searching and detection in the days before electronics was a complete waste of time, land having long since disappeared beyond the horizon. Recent expeditions to the area, using electronic navigation systems and magnetometers, revealed several new wrecks over a long weekend. Such is our potential today.

In order to successfully find wrecks, a team needs to use both electronic navigation systems and proton magnetometers together, as well as a reliable echo sounder. In some cases, the magnetometer is surplus to requirements, particularly if the wreck's charted position is known to be accurate.

Let us assume two situations not uncommon in the art of wreck detection. In the first we have an accurate chart position of the site, and in the second we only have a 'position approximate' for the target site.

In both these situations we would programme each position into the Decca Navigator as a waypoint. The former, of course, will be more accurately pinpointed as we will be able to programme in degrees, minutes and hundredths, whereas a 'position approximate' will be minus the hundredths.

Having set our waypoint, the computer will give us a course to steer, as well as a distance off the site and a time prediction before we get there. As we approach the site the waypoint alarm warns of our impending approach, and it is time for concentration on the final search. It is possible to keep the normal latitude and longitude display on the computer until the machine says we are there; then we should have a large datum buoy ready to throw over. This gives a point from which a systematic search using the echo sounder can be made.

An even more accurate final approach can be made by adjusting the machine to give positions using the coloured Decca lanes. By driving down one of the lanes, rather like driving along a transit-bearing position line, one can wait until the other co-ordinate matches the predicted position and then throw in the datum marker. If the Decca is programmed very accurately and there is no signal error, the wreck may 'show' without having to search any further. (See Figure 86.) When looking for a new wreck, it is usually necessary to start a systematic search away from the datum buoy. A second marker buoy needs to be rigged ready to be thrown in once the sounder trace shows an anomaly. The first one can then be retrieved and used again if the skipper decides to pick out any more 'high spots' using the sounder in further sweeps around the site. This all sounds very straightforward and simple, which in theory it is. Much depends, however, on the nature of the sea bed and whether the wreck stands proud, or is hidden somewhat in a depression or gully. A well-flattened wreck will still have one or two large lumps to identify it, the engines, boilers, etc., and these may take some time before being located.

Always allow plenty of searching time if you are planning to dive on a site where slack tide is necessary, as it is surprising how quickly time disappears. One can be frustratingly close to the site, missing prominent pieces of wreckage by only a few metres, as one steams slowly up and down, eyes willing the needle on the sounder to suddenly shoot up the trace.

Once the wreck is positively located it is important to take accurate Decca positions, which are then unique to your machine. Future trips should then produce no navigational problems.

In the second situation outlined above, the use of a proton magnetometer will be necessary. (See Figure 87.) One needs to understand a little about how the magnetometer works, as search techniques are influenced by this. In simple terms the earth is a huge magnet with magnetic lines of force connecting both the North Pole and the South Pole in a similar fashion to the lines of force present on a bar magnet. Any large metal object, like a

shipwreck on the sea bed, will create a local magnetic anomaly and alter the earth's magnetic field slightly around the immediate area. The magnetometer is a device capable of detecting such anomalies. It consists of a control box (Figure 88) and a length of cable attached to a sensory 'fish' (Figure 89) which is trawled behind the towing boat. There needs to be a sufficient length of cable to avoid false signals due to the wash of the boat. Its effectiveness also depends on the depth and the size of the wreckage below. Large lumps will obviously be more detectable than small ones. Magnetometers are usually supplied with a 'sensitivity' graph with which it is possible to calculate a maximum 'sensing' distance, and thus decide on the size of each search lane. A weighted fish towed in mid-water is more effective than one towed just beneath the surface. Care must be taken not to tow too deep, however, as you could snag the fish in the wreck.

The magnetometer is adjusted so that the audible sound pulse is set for a 'no anomaly' situation. As the earth's magnetic pattern alters, it is important to ensure the machine is monitoring the area you are operating in. The fish is then towed behind the boat, and any anomaly will be detected by a quickening and increased sound level of the audible signal. The needle on the control box also indicates when an anomaly is present, going off the scale when large pieces of wreckage are located. The audible signal will screech in this situation. It is important that at least one member of the search team is experienced, as the practised ear can tell well in advance

Figure 86 Echo sounder trace of a large wreck

Figure 87 Proton magnetometer

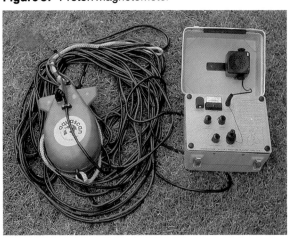

when things start to happen. Expert users can even estimate accurately how big each lump of wreckage is. A large intact wreck, for example, will give an indication some distance away which will build up to a peak over the wreck and then die away again. A scattered or broken wreck will tend to give multiple changes and peaks in the signal. Small objects like cannons will only give a momentary change in the signal. It takes a practised ear to differentiate these signals. One tried and tested method of marking out the site (see Figure 92) is to lay an initial datum buoy and approach the area around this on a number of different and reciprocal bearings. Further marker buoys are dropped at the point of detection on each bearing. A pattern of about eight marker buoys gives quite a good impression of both the size and distribution of the wreck.

The theory of how magnetometers work and how this can affect their practical use has been mentioned above. Figure 93 shows a wreck site and the way in which local magnetic lines of force are distorted. As you can see, the effect of the wreck is to exaggerate and elongate the lines of force north and south, and not as much east and west. It is logical, therefore, to steam courses east and west, as the wreck site will provide a much bigger 'target' than a north-to-south, south-to-north search pattern. Sensing, however, occurs both vertically and horizontally.

In the second situation we would use the Decca Navigator to achieve a position where we could deploy a datum buoy, which should be large enough to be seen from long distances. A 'dan buoy', with a prominent pole and flag attached standing 3 metres above the surface of the sea, would be ideal. With the datum buoy in position, the search pattern can begin. As in any search, it is vital that 100 per cent of the area is covered and a record of it is kept. Towing the magnetometer fish at a reasonable speed, we would steam east and west either side of the datum buoy. We could decide on the 'boxes' to be searched and plot their position on the chart.

Figure 94 shows another example of a search pattern. Each change of direction can be set using compass headings and timing each leg. Alternatively, position changes on the Decca could guide the helmsman. Once again, co-ordinated teamwork is essential. One person needs to steer the vessel along an accurate course while another tends the Decca Navigator, constantly monitoring position and liaising closely with the helmsman. The magnetometer operator needs to maintain a constant surveillance on his instruments, and have instant communication to the bridge if the instrument is deployed on deck. A series of marker buoys need to be instantly deployable once the magnetometer becomes active. When this happens, the ship's position should be registered, perhaps using the Decca's 'man overboard' facility, to give an instantly programmed waypoint. A buoy can be thrown in, and the ship circle it looking for the strongest reading. The echo sounder can be switched on for tell-tale signs on the trace. Expert magnetometer users can trace the whole wreck site in terms of extent and size even before anyone dives the site.

An alternative search method (see Figure 91) uses tidal flow and a small boat. As can be seen, the fish is suspended from the boat which is allowed to drift with the tidal stream. A marker buoy locates the start of the run, and after a pre-determined distance has been covered, perhaps using time as the guide, a second marker buoy sets the end of the area covered. The fish is then retrieved, and the boat returns to the start line to

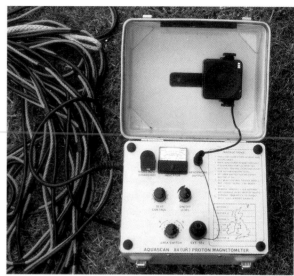

Figure 88 Magnetometer control box

Figure 89 Magnetometer 'fish'

Figure 90 Needle actuated by wreck position

begin a parallel course.

Once the site has been confirmed, divers should avoid pulling themselves down the buoyline until it has been securely tied in. There is nothing more frustrating than to find that the shot has been dragged out of the wreck by the vigorous pulling actions of divers striving to get to the bottom.

All of this section has concentrated on modern methods of wreck detection. In certain conditions, however, those without use of the above equipment can successfully search large areas of the sea bed using an aquaplane towed by a boat. This is an old, but potentially efficient method of wreck searching, as well as being exhilarating for the divers involved. Figure 109 shows a two-person aquaplane which the divers can control for up and down movement by weight transfer on the leading edge.

This method of search is only successful if certain conditions are met. The operating depth should not exceed 20 metres, and good visibility is needed to ensure that underwater obstructions are easily located. A method of marking any site should be planned with the understanding of the cover boat crew. Once a find is located, both divers can roll off the aquaplane. A crew member holding the tow line will feel the weight go off it and react accordingly. Alternatively, the divers could release a small buoy if they wished to explore their find further, enabling the surface boat to locate them.

Wreck detection using this technique relies on the expertise of the boat crew to systematically search areas of the sea bed without any omission. The aquaplane requires careful design, preferably allowing the divers to hold on to the board without relying on arm strength alone as they can get very tired. Lead weights may be needed on the front of the aquaplane to ensure it 'dives' easily. In cooler water temperatures, dry suits are recommended. Decompression times should also be carefully monitored. Divers engaged in such passive activities do not use as much air, and it is very easy to lose track of time and depth.

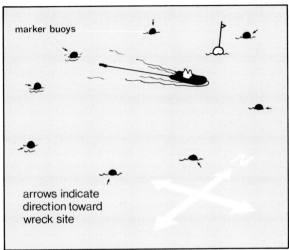

Figure 92 Marker buoys outlining site profile

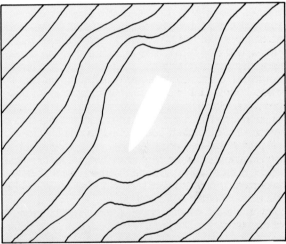

Figure 93 Lines of magnetic force

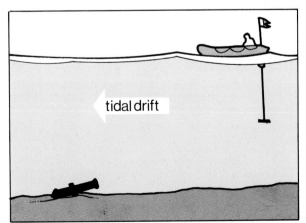

Figure 91 'Fish' suspended from a small boat
Figure 94 Typical search pattern using a compass heading

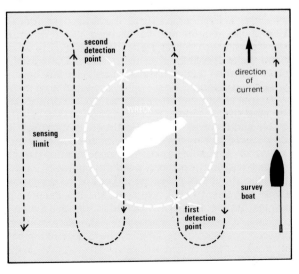

Wreck Penetration

Exploration of the inside of a wreck can be very rewarding; however, as with any 'no clear surface' diving, it is potentially very hazardous. What appears to be an easily accessible entrance with good visibility can quickly turn into a zero visibility death trap. Wreck penetration requires proper planning, preparation, and equipment. Divers with a strong interest in the topic will see similarities to cave diving and should read the relevant section in this book. This type of dive can be divided into three general categories, though there will be an overlap between them. No type of wreck penetration dive should be undertaken unless all the divers concerned have the appropriate experience, and adequate pre-dive planning and preparation has taken place.

No clear surface

This category generally applies when diving broken-up wrecks. The diver is presented with a section of wreckage under which he may clearly swim, but in the course of doing so his clear access to the surface will be obstructed. The seriousness of such action will depend upon a number of factors – distance, size of aperture, degree of silting, and general visibility. In the simplest cases both leader and buddy may simply swim under that section and out into clear water. In other cases problems created by the above factors will need to be anticipated and solved. More formal buddy checks must be performed, and consideration given to whether the more experienced or less experienced diver should lead this section. Bear in mind that the second of the pair may have to contend with reduced visibility caused by the passage of the first diver.

If there is silt, swimming well above it may be possible, or alternatively, make progress without finning by pulling yourself with your hands. Perfect buoyancy control is an essential factor in all types of wreck penetration if correct positioning of the diver is to be achieved. Another possible problem will occur if the divers are using a bottom line from the shot. In this case, the leader must decide whether the pair are to be committed to swimming under this section on their return. The use of a surface marker buoy will also complicate this type of wreck penetration.

As with all types of wreck penetration, the divers must be sure that any portion of wreckage above them is stable and not likely to fall. Unstable wreckage may be dislodged either by the actions of the group penetrating the wreck, or possibly by other groups exploring the site. In very unstable conditions, even the buoyancy caused by exhaust bubbles collecting in parts of the wreck can cause movement. Other dive boats arriving and anchoring into the wreck have also caused incidents in the past.

Figure 95 Diver on a large wreck

Vertical penetration

This is where the divers descend vertically into a section of wreck which initially has clear surface access. This situation frequently occurs in upright wrecks where hold covers, wooden decking or engine-room skylights have disappeared. The main problem which then occurs is the temptation to move horizontally under overhanging decks into darker recesses. In this situation the divers will usually need to return to their original point of entry. This may be possible by simple navigation/orientation or may mean the use of a bottom line. Lower decks are frequently silt covered, and visibility can quickly be reduced to zero by careless finning or even by the deployment of the bottom line.

Entry into very dark spaces is pointless without a good torch, and in more serious cases safety will be compromised unless both divers are so equipped. It is also possible inadvertently to exceed planned depth limits in this type of dive, as wrecks frequently settle into soft sea beds. In the bottom of holds or engine rooms the diver may encounter depths below that of the surrounding sea bed.

Extended penetration

The third category of penetration dive is even more hazardous, involving exploration of very enclosed areas such as gun turrets, companionways, bridges and cabins. Here detailed planning is usually essential, and experience gained in the first two categories will pay dividends. All the problems mentioned before are now amplified, and are even more difficult to resolve. When planning air requirements for the dive, only a proportion of the total air supply will be allocated to the penetration. Divers should plan to finish exploration when one-third of this portion of air supply has been used, leaving two-thirds for the exit phase.

Some knowledge of the route to be followed is more than helpful in the planning stage. Obviously, this is where previous orientation experience, both above and below the surface, will prove useful. In some cases the divers may be able to gain access to the plans of the ship to be dived, or even to explore a still floating sister ship.

It may well be appropriate for the buddy to remain outside tending the leader as a roped diver. This means the leader must cope with any problems virtually alone, although this situation may be safer than the additional problems caused by the presence of two divers in very confined spaces. If this technique is to be adopted, then it is obvious that the pair should have previously operated together as tender and roped diver in a clear-water situation. Any extended penetration needs some form of bottom line as a guide back to the exit; this can be vital on even short penetrations as the visibility can quickly be reduced by silt clouds.

Besides the main working lamp an additional small emergency torch is a sensible precaution. Correct neutral buoyancy is essential to minimize silt disturbance, together with movement skills such as 'finger walking' and 'single finning' (single finning is using the 'top' fin only for propulsion, the lower fin shielding the silt). All possible precautions to streamline equipment and avoid snagging should be taken. Divers should even consider whether a snorkel is an appropriate accessory for this type of dive.

The first look into an enclosed space usually occurs with torch and head first, but if access is very restricted it may not be a good idea to continue this type of entry too far. If the diver should become snagged on exit, unaided extrication is very difficult. Following the initial examination it may be better to use a fins-first entry. This makes retreat simpler, and has the added bonus of giving the conger a chew at your fins rather than your face! Any form of entry that requires removal of equipment and subsequent re-kitting inside the wreck is to be avoided. Rapid exit in an emergency is an important criterion to measure against the reasons for entering any wreck.

The diver or divers penetrating the wreck must adhere to the dive plan, and any cover divers outside must know and understand the plan. Beware of thinking that bubbles emerging from the wreck are a sign that divers inside are not in difficulty, as exhaust air can take hours to trickle out. If the divers in the wreck are overdue, rescue plans should be put into effect immediately.

Figure 96 Moody wreck site

Orientation

Actually understanding where you are on a wreck, even when it is relatively intact, can be quite a problem to many would-be wreck divers. This can do more than reduce the enjoyment or usefulness of the diver, as failure to navigate amongst the wreckage can also mean failure to regain the shotline for the ascent.

There are two simple steps which can be taken to reduce this problem. The first is to gain as much first-hand knowledge of underwater pilotage as possible. This will involve experience gathered over a number of dives at a variety of sites, usually acting as the dive leader. Navigation over a route by means of recognized objects, rather than compass navigation, is the most useful skill. Indeed, the use of a compass for navigating is frequently compromised when exploring wrecks which consist of large masses of iron and steel.

The second step does not even require the diver to get wet! Take every opportunity to explore ships on the surface, either first hand or through books, photographs and drawings. Some tact is needed when visiting engine rooms and bridges – discussing the real reason for the visit does not always go down too well with the crew!

This research is never wasted and, besides making navigation on the wreck easier, will also pay dividends when trying to locate particular areas of the ship. Most

Figure 98 Shipwreck showing empty bow section

divers find the bridge, accommodation and engine rooms interesting places to visit, and recognizing features such as the anchor chain and understanding it is normally stored in the bows will certainly help. Few wrecks actually resemble a ship – most look like a badly kept scrap heap seen on a very foggy day. This is especially true of the shallower, more accessible wrecks

Figure 97 Ship's engine room

because of the increased damage caused by wave action. Finding items such as navigation instruments, telegraphs, etc., can indicate the proximity of the bridge and officers' quarters. Crockery and cutlery may help locate the galley or crew's quarters, depending on the type of ship. Engine and boiler rooms are often the most easily identifiable areas, because of the solid construction of these items. On well-dispersed wrecks frequently the most recognizable parts are the engines, prop shaft and propeller (if it was ferrous). Unless the ship was carrying a particularly interesting cargo, holds are usually not very exciting areas and are rather devoid of the non-ferrous objects divers like to observe. (See Figure 98.)

As a wreck site becomes better known to a diver, more accurate surface-position fixing may become possible. On many larger wrecks good use of transits, for example, may mean the shot can be accurately placed in a particular section of the wreck, such as the engine room. This kind of knowledge can save a lot of valuable underwater time by allowing the divers to swim straight down to the portion of the wreck they wish to work on or explore.

On a first visit to a wreck many divers concentrate on a 'grand tour', attempting to get an overall picture of the site. Indeed, on larger wrecks this may take more than

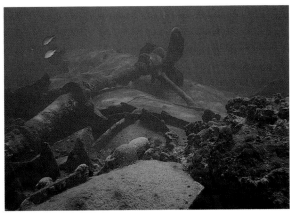

Figure 99 Wreck in clear water

one dive. Once significant features have been identified, it is often possible to produce a sketch outlining the layout of the wreck. The input of other dive groups can often help build up details more rapidly. These sketches can be very useful in directing diving groups in further exploration of the site, and even in positive identification of the wreck. (See Figure 100.)

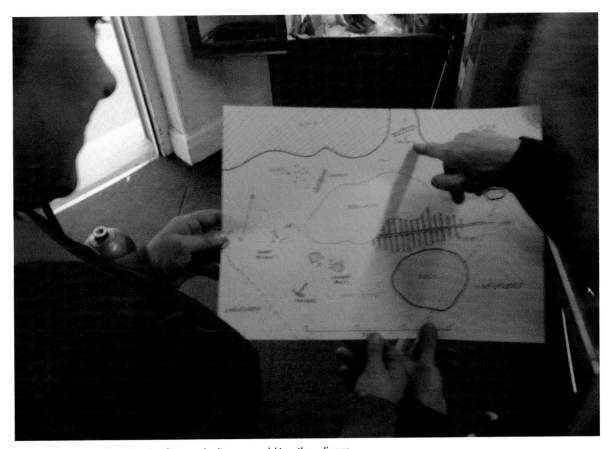

Figure 100 Detailed sketch of a wreck site as an aid to other divers

Diving Statistics

Exact statistics about all manner of diving activities are very difficult to quantify as it is impossible to monitor, for example, how many dives take place in a particular location over a twelve-month period.

Statistics relevant to diving activities fit into specific areas.

All safety-conscious diving organizations, such as the BSAC, are obviously interested in diving accidents and incidents and any trends that can be determined from their analysis.

Diving equipment manufacturers are interested in trends in equipment use and preference in terms of their future products. The move from an established or traditional product towards a later development must be followed closely in order to ensure that the products available on the market match as closely as possible the needs of the market.

Organizations connected with the promotion of the sport will be interested in the range of people taking part in the sport. In countries like the UK, with less than ideal weather and colder waters, only about 12 per cent of sport divers are female. In Japan, however, with kinder environmental conditions and the upsurge of career women with good incomes, more than 50 per cent of new divers are female.

Of the above areas of interest the most predominant seems to be the area of accidents and incidents, since this is often the area of public interest.

For many years the BSAC has analysed diving incidents in the UK, along with a few overseas incidents involving BSAC members. Each year a comprehensive report is published giving brief details of each reported incident and a full analysis of trends. Incidents are divided into categories such as Fatalities, Decompression Sickness, Boating Incidents, etc. Very few other organizations involved with the sport collect such data, another notable example being the Divers Alert Network (DAN) in the USA.

Incidents data is collected and collated from various sources in order to maximize data capture. Members of BSAC branches and diving schools are encouraged to submit incident reports if they are unfortunate enough to be involved in one. Names are never disclosed to ensure confidentiality and to encourage divers to be forthcoming with information. Reports are used to recognize and analyse trends, which can then be given maximum publicity, in order to help avoid future incidents.

Data is also supplied by HM Coastguard Service, who provide duplicate Coastguard Rescue Incident Reports for any case they deal with which involves amateur divers around the shores of the UK. Many recompression chambers also provide dive profiles and other relevant information for all cases of decompression sickness they treat. Newspaper articles often provide preliminary information relating to diving accidents and incidents.

Incidents involving divers inevitably lead to media reports, sometimes of a sensationalist nature, and these can give the sport poor publicity. The BSAC has always tried to maintain a balanced view when analysing figures and to place in perspective figures which on first inspection might seem to be disturbing. Over recent years there have been approximately 100 cases of decompression sickness over a 12-month period. A conservative estimate of 1,000,000 dives takes place over the same period, which gives a risk of 0.01 per cent of a diver suffering from decompression sickness. An average figure of 15 fatalities has occurred per year over the same time span, which gives a risk of 0.0015 per cent, which suggests that one has about an equal percentage chance of dying whilst diving as when driving a car.

In spite of these relatively low risk factors and the fact that the sport has been described as one for 'active grandmothers', it is still regarded by the ill-informed as being dangerous. In a recent survey of 'The Ten Most Dangerous Sports' diving was not even mentioned in the list, which was as follows:

1. Motor Racing (Car and Bike)
2. Horse Riding
3. Mountain/Rock Climbing
4. Fishing
5. Gliding/Hang Gliding
6. Canoeing and Sailing
7. Soccer/Rugby
8. Athletics/Jogging
9. Cycling
10. Martial Arts/Boxing.

Figure 101 BSAC incident report form

Incident/Accident Report Form — (In Confidence)

Details of incident and any action taken: (Use another sheet of paper if more space is required).
Equipment. Indicate type, model and condition before and after dive. Also cylinder capacity(ies) and amount of weight carried.

British Sub-Aqua Club
Incident/Accident Report Form

Relevant incident factors must be indicated in the column below

Brief summary of incident e.g. Fatality; Bend; Lost Divers

Date and place of inquest(s)

Diver(s) directly involved

A Name — Age

Membership No. — Club/Branch

Physical condition, recently and on day of incident. Indicate any physical incapacity.

Next of Kin

B Name — Age

Membership No. — Club/Branch

Physical conditions, recently and on day of incident. Indicate any physical incapacity.

Next of Kin.

Dive details

Organising Club/Branch

Location

Date	Time	Weather
Sea conditions	Surface visibility	Underwater visibility

Maximum depth	Dive 1	Dive 2	Dive 3
Bottom time			
Surface interval			

Particulars of any dives in the previous 24 hours

In the event of decompression having been carried out, list stops made

Dive 1	mins @	m	mins @	m	Total ascent time
Dive 2	mins @	m	mins @	m	Total ascent time
Dive 3	mins @	m	mins @	m	Total ascent time

In the event of recompression having been carried out, state where

INSERT APPLICABLE CODE LETTERS Use X if unknown or not relevant	Diver A	Diver B
MEMBERSHIP B BSAC, I Independent, O No organisation, C Commercial, N National Snorkellers Club		
QUALIFICATIONS O None, S Snorkeller, N Novice, Sp Sports Diver, DL Dive Leader, A Advanced Diver, 1 1st Class, I Instructor		
ORGANISATION OF DIVE C Club/Branch, P Private, Comm Commercial, H Holiday		
TYPE OF DIVE B Boat, Sh Shore, Sn Snorkel, D Drift, T Training Drill, O None, W Wreck, X Cold, Y Deep, Z Decompression		
LOCALITY H Home, A Abroad, F Freshwater, S Sea, L Land, P Swimming Pool		
DEPTH IN METRES		

Please circle relevant code(s)
Code Factor

INJURY/ILLNESS
01 Fatality
02 Embolism
03 Decompression Sickness
04 Injury
05 Illness
06 Ear problems/damage
07 Hypothermia
08 Unconsciousness
09 Resuscitation Involved
10 Breathlessness
11 Narcosis

TECHNIQUE
12 Aborted Dive
13 Assisted Ascent
14 Buoyant Ascent
15 Free Ascent
16 Other Ascent
17 Lost diver(s)
18 Buoyancy/weight
19 Carelessness
20 Ignorance
21 Disregard of rules
22 Malice
23 Out of Air
24 Pre-dive check
25 Rough water
26 Bad seamanship
27 Good seamanship
28 Good practice
29 Separation
30 Trio diving
31 Training drill
32 Training inadequate
33 Sharing
34 Deep dive (30m+)
35 Low U/W Vis.
36 Low Surface Vis.
37 False alarm
38 Solo dive
39 Divers underwater
40 Diver on surface
41 Nets
42 Cold water

EQUIPMENT
43 Boat problems
44 Motor problems
45 Reg. Performance
46 Equipment faulty
47 Equipment fitting
48 Equipment use
49 Equipment wear
50 Equipment inadequate
51 Ropes
52 SMB absent
53 SMB inadequate
54 SMB contributed
55 Propellor
56 ABLJ/BC
57 Dry suit

CHANCE
58 Fire/explosion
59 Foul air

RESCUE SERVICES
60 Ambulance
61 Police
62 Helicopter
63 Coastguard
64 Lifeboat

DECOMPRESSION SICKNESS ANALYSIS
65 Recomp./Chamber
66 Recomp./U/W
67 Within Tables
68 Rapid Ascent
69 Repeat diving
70 Deep diving (40m+)
71 BSAC tables
72 Inaccurate use/tables

Complete this form with as much information as possible and return to BSAC HQ **WITHOUT DELAY**

Underwater Techniques

Search Methods

Underwater searching is a skill which requires a team of competent divers if it is to be fully successful. Underwater search methods and techniques are taught by the BSAC as part of its diver training programme, but relatively few divers actually look for objects after their initial training using the techniques taught.

For those who do get involved, the more common objects which they might be required to look for include lobster pots which have become stuck in wreckage, and outboard motors which have been lost. At one time, local diving clubs would be enlisted by the police in order to conduct underwater searches for missing persons, presumed drowned. Fortunately, all police forces now have the use of their own specialist underwater search units who carry out these less than pleasant tasks.

Although many search techniques are theoretically simple, to be successful it is preferable for a team of divers to work together regularly, as co-ordination and teamwork are vital to ensure success. A system of rope signals needs to be worked out for those search techniques which involve divers on a line. 'Pulls' and 'bells' need to be fully understood, and there is a lot to be said for training would-be search divers in the pool, using blacked-out masks, etc., in order that they may get used to relying on signals for communication underwater. Many a simple plan has gone badly wrong once the divers find themselves disorientated, perhaps underweighted, and wrapped in surplus line in the murk of an open-water search location.

Thought must be given to the types of rope and line to be used in searching, and how they are to be deployed underwater. Most modern ropes made out of material like polypropylene float, and may need to be weighted at regular intervals if they are to be deployed as fixed bottom lines. Reels are useful devices to avoid tangles underwater. SMB reels, with thin line which is often negatively buoyant, can double as equipment for laying fixed 'jackstays'. Others may prefer to use purpose-built reels for similar operations.

Before going into the details of different search techniques, it is worthwhile looking at the parameters necessary for any successful search:

a. Make it simple
The simpler the technique employed, the less there is to go wrong, and the easier it is to train divers in the method. Time is all important, and no one wants to waste it by learning complicated manoeuvres.

b. It must be effective
Effectiveness can be measured in terms of the cost and effort involved. The whole project should be assessed, from the planning phase through to the actual execution. Obviously, this will depend on the scale of the operation. Are we looking for a gold ring dropped from a pier in a known location, or are we looking for a valuable wristwatch dropped from a moving boat in an uncertain location? It is very unlikely, however, that the object will be found close to the datum position. The search needs to cover the determined search area as quickly and as effectively as possible.

c. 100 per cent coverage is essential
Any search which does not cover 100 per cent of the designated area is pointless. As mentioned above, it is very rare for the object to lie next to the initial datum position. A systematic search away from this point must tell the searchers where the object is not, and areas need eliminating as the search progresses. There is nothing worse than to be unsure whether an area has been fully searched.

d. Navigation problems need to be reduced to a minimum
If a relatively large area is to be covered, the problems of navigation and the effects of wind and/or tide are a prime consideration. Electronic navigation systems now available can give a high degree of accuracy in terms of determining a vessel's position if the search area is a large one. Constant checking is an absolute must if wind and tide are strong enough to interfere with the divers' performance underwater.

e. Adaptability is essential
Any search method may prove to be unsuitable once the bottom conditions become evident. A circular search technique, for example, may be rendered completely ineffective because of the presence of a large area of kelp. Divers need to be constantly aware of the need to adapt to the conditions and, if necessary, change their techniques accordingly.

There are several search techniques in general use. Nearly all use rope in some form or another. Some rely on boats, either to move divers around or to set up search boundaries. All rely on planning and good execution.

Search techniques may be listed as follows:

a Free swim with two or more divers, using a compass to navigate underwater.

b Swimline/dragline search in a restricted area.

c Swimline search in the open sea.

d Circular search around a heavy shot and surface line and circular search variations of technique for a badly obstructed bottom.

e Pendulum or swing search using the shoreline as end datum markers.

f Fixed line or jackstay searches of various types, using swimlines either to locate or snag underwater objects.

g Towed diver searches using a boat.

Free-swim compass search

This technique is best suited to searching for large objects in conditions of good visibility. It relies on the divers' underwater navigational skills using a compass, but the accuracy of the search also depends on other factors, such as the effects of tidal streams pushing the divers off their predicted route. Different search patterns can be adopted, as illustrated in Figure 102. The square spiral pattern needs to have a method for determining the length of each leg swum. In a free-swimming situation this will either involve counting fin strokes or timing. If you use the timing method it would be useful for the divers to know how many metres they would cover in, for example, ten seconds in order to plan realistic legs. Any sort of water movement would, of course, throw into disarray such calculations. Slack-water conditions are thus vital for any degree of accuracy using a free-swim technique.

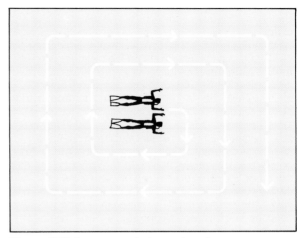

Figure 102 A square spiral search pattern

Swimline/dragline search in a restricted area

This technique is best suited to searching areas of water like rivers or canals, where there is restricted water area and the banks or the river/canal act as limits to the area searched. As Figure 103 shows, the two divers on the ends of the line keep the line taut and are responsible for keeping the rope stretched between the river banks. The other divers on the line need to be spaced out at regular intervals, the distance being determined by the underwater visibility. If a river is being searched one needs to take a decision about the use of the current, and whether to swim with it or against it. To swim with it is most economical in terms of expending divers' energy. Problems can arise, however, with a soft muddy bottom which stirs up as the swimline and the divers pass over it. This has the effect of creating even worse underwater visibility. Provided the current is not too strong, it may be prudent to work against it, and thus allow stirred-up sediment to be washed away from the divers.

This technique can be adapted to the open sea when an area is boxed off using fixed jackstays, parallel to each other. Figure 104 illustrates this, with each of the divers swimming down the jackstay and using the weighted line as a snagline between them.

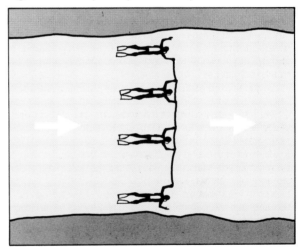

Figure 103 Search method for restricted waters

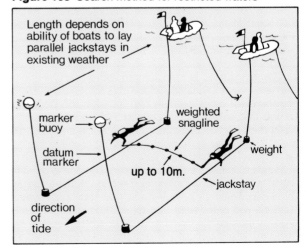

Length depends on ability of boats to lay parallel jackstays in existing weather

marker buoy

datum marker

weighted snagline

up to 10m.

weight

jackstay

direction of tide

Figure 104 A seabed snag-line search

Swimline search in the open sea

The basis of this technique is to lay a fixed datum line, or jackstay, from a boat. The line is weighted and buoyed at each end. The team of divers then descends at one end of the datum line using a swimline, which is deployed at right angles to the jackstay. With a well-trained team it is possible to have many divers on the swimline, depending on underwater visibility and surface conditions. A swimline controller would be positioned in the middle of the line, with the end divers carrying surface marker buoys. Figure 106 shows the configuration for the swim. Once the search has proceeded to the end of the datum line, another line is laid parallel to the first. To ensure 100 per cent coverage there will be a built-in overlap between search areas. This method, perhaps more than any other, requires reliable and efficient teamwork, both between the divers, and between the divers and the boat crews. Boat crews must be constantly alert for signs of difficulty and distress, especially if large numbers of divers are in the water.

Circular search

The circular search technique around a central weighted shotline is often the easiest to set up with the equipment divers normally have available. It is not difficult to understand and is the method most commonly adopted in training drills.

As the search pattern is obviously circular, the technique is most effective where an accurate fix on the lost object has been acquired. If a wide area is to be covered there needs to be an overlap in order to avoid leaving large areas of the bottom unsearched. (See Figure 107.) It is also best used on an unobstructed bottom, as kelp or large boulders will continually snag the search line and render operations impossible. Because the swimline needs to be kept taut, there is a limit to how far out from the shotline the search may be extended. The absolute maximum is 20 metres, with 15 metres being a more realistic figure. Figure 105 shows the layout for a typical circular search pattern. The shotline needs to have a shotweight heavy enough to prevent the divers dragging it as they complete their circles. Divers sometimes forget that a taut shotline on a large surface buoy will have the effect of lifting the shotweight, especially if there is surface swell. Ideally, the shotweight should weigh 25 kilograms.

The divers need to be equipped with a reel and line to be used as a swimline, which should ideally have a carabiner or other suitable clip allowing the divers to attach themselves to the bottom of the shotline easily. SMB reels are useful for this purpose as the line does not need to be large in diameter. It may be useful to mark it at regular intervals with tape in order to determine accurate distance away from the shot. The divers need to have some means of marking the find, either using an SMB carried by the outside diver, or a small buoy which is deployed only when the object is found. The latter system reduces the number of lines which need to be handled. Many a circular search has been hampered by the SMB either becoming entangled in the swimline or distracting the diver carrying it to the extent that he forgets to keep the swimline taut.

All circular search techniques need some way of indicating that a complete revolution around the shot has been made. By far the most effective method is that shown in Figure 105. A fixed bottom line is laid out in a straight line from the shot, the length of which will be the limit of the search. Each time the divers reach this line they know they need to increase the radius of their search and move out along the swimline. Some may prefer to mark regular distances on this bottom line rather than the swimline, and use the datum line to determine how far to move out. Underwater visibility will, of course, determine the radius to be swept.

A very popular method of marking a complete circle is to use a movable marker. This is relocated by the outside diver each time a revolution is completed. If the bottom is suitably soft a metal spike could be used. Never use a wooden spike – it may float away. If you decide to use a marker, it is far better to use a small weight with a metre length of thin line attached. A small polythene bottle filled with enough air to float the bottle *without raising the weight* is then tied to the line. This has the advantage of being able to be used on a firm bottom, being easily movable and visible.

The fixed datum line, however, is much more failsafe in the sense that it cannot be missed in poor visibility. A movable marker at the outward limit of the search can easily be missed in poor visibility if the swimline for any reason becomes less than taut and the divers finish their circumnavigation with less of a radius than the one they started with.

An alternative to the standard circular search may be necessary in a location where submerged obstructions such as trees, boulders and thick kelp render standard operations impossible. Figure 108 shows the 'pie method'. The shotline is located at the centre of the search area and a fixed datum line is laid out from the shot, determining the radius. Divers then swim along one side of the line, turn round, and swim down the other side. The datum line is then moved around to another position, the distance being determined by the visibility. The divers gradually work their way around the shotline through 360 degrees.

Figure 105 Circular search. This is the simplest method of searching the seabed. Particularly useful for locating small objects in poor visibility

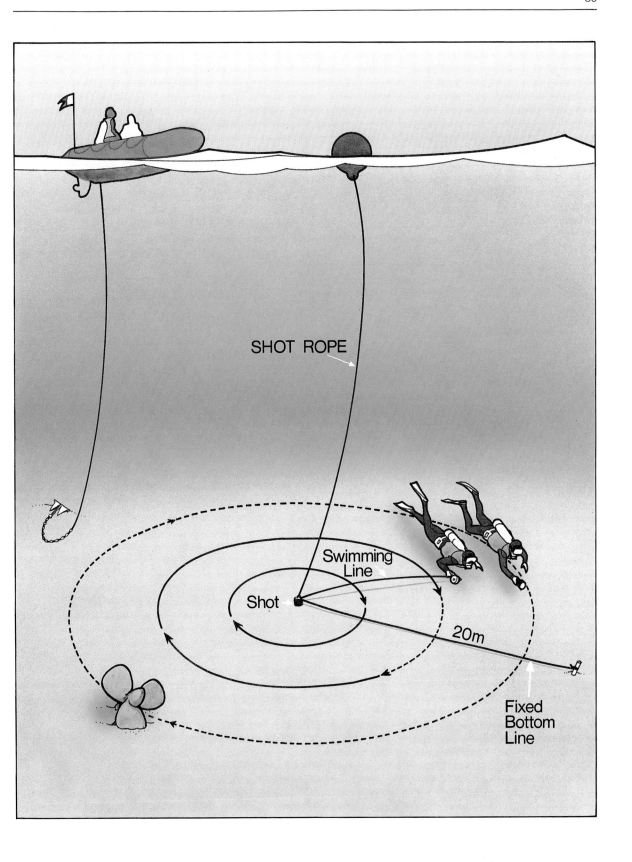

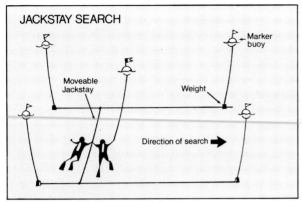

Figure 106 A jackstay search

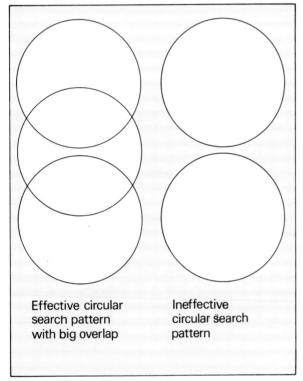

Figure 107 Circular search patterns

Pendulum or swing search

The pendulum or swing search is an adaptation from the circular search technique and, to be successful, the area to be covered needs to be off the shore, as shown in Figure 110. It is necessary for the line to be fixed to a point on the shore. The divers keep the line taut and use the shore as datum points, swimming in a pendulum pattern in ever-increasing distances away from it. There are two ways of achieving this. The line can be fixed to a stake or other suitable object, and the divers can be responsible for reeling out line as they come to the end of each sweep. The alternative is for the divers to hold the end of the line, while a surface tender is responsible for paying out a predetermined amount of line at the end of each sweep. A suitably marked line is necessary for the latter.

Fixed line or jackstay searches

A jackstay is a line fixed to the bottom by weights and used as a datum point for searching. A jackstay can be fixed or movable, according to the search method used. The grid search employs both fixed and movable jackstays. Figure 111 shows how this is achieved. Two parallel fixed jackstays are laid, weighted, and the four corners of the 'box' buoyed at the surface. A movable jackstay is deployed at right angles to the fixed lines. Divers swim up one side of the movable jackstay and down the other. The jackstay is then moved along a suitable distance, incorporating an overlap, and the process repeated. This is a good search technique to use when looking for small objects in a restricted area. A further extension of this is to lay fixed jackstays between the two long jackstays, instead of using the movable jackstays. This method ensures a high degree of accuracy, but involves a large amount of rope and a lot of experience in deploying it. It all sounds simple in theory, but to execute the task in a heaving sea with wind affecting the positions of the boats is difficult and requires plenty of practice.

All the above search methods need practice before they can be executed efficiently. It is recommended that divers become familiar with techniques, which may involve dry runs on shore. This will ensure that each diver knows his or her task in the water, the rope signals which may be involved, and becomes confident with each aspect of the operation.

Towed diver searches using a boat

When searching for a large object in conditions of good visibility, divers may be towed by an aquaplane behind a boat. This technique is more fully described in 'Wreck Detection', p. 68.

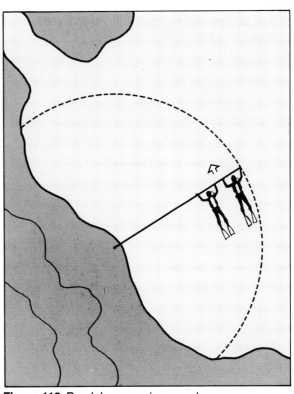

Figure 108 'Pie' search method

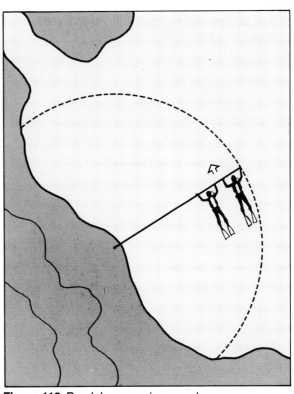

Figure 110 Pendulum or swing search

Figure 109 Home made aquaplane

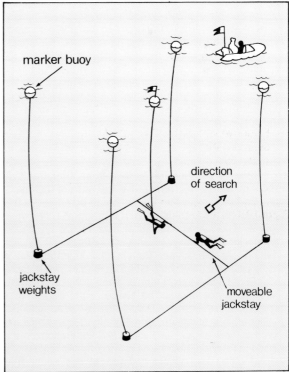

Figure 111 Fixed jackstay search

Underwater Lifting

While seeking an outlet for their diving skills, many groups of divers turn towards lifting exercises and similar projects which can be most satisfying underwater experiences. The development of suitable equipment and the widespread use of boats has made lifting projects both possible and within the scope of amateur divers.

The use of compressed air for lifting heavy objects was pioneered by the famous salvage company of Cox & Danks (Metal Industries) in the Scapa Flow, Orkney, during the 1920s. Their salvage of all but seven of the seventy-four vessels of the German High Seas Fleet, which were scuttled in up to 50 metres of water following their internment at the end of World War I, saw the successful use of compressed air to lift 'Dreadnought' battleships of up to 26,000 tonnes. Divers fitted airlocks to the submerged hulls, many of which were inverted, and workers were able to descend inside the vessels to plug any holes. Compressed air was pumped inside them and, contrary to the views of sceptics, the operations were a huge success. In all the years of salvage prior to this success, nearly all ocean salvage had relied on mechanical methods.

Amateur divers, of course, are naturally equipped for using compressed air for lifting, and this section covers the practical ways in which lifting projects can be organized. Successful projects carried out by teams of amateur divers are referred to and serve as models for future schemes.

The principle of lifting objects using air is very simple. A litre of water weighs 1 kilogram, so that if you displace 1 litre of water with air, you will have gained 1 kilogram of positive buoyancy. Thus, an object weighing 60 kilograms will require 60 litres of air at ambient pressure in order to lift it. Boyle's Law affects how much 'free air' you will need according to the operating depth. A 60 kilogram object will only require 60 litres of air at the surface pressure of 1 bar, but would require 240 litres at 30 metres when the pressure had quadrupled. A lifting bag completely full of air and capable of lifting a 60 kilogram object would thus 'lose' 180 litres of surplus air by the time it reached the surface from 30 metres (240 litres – 60 litres = 180 litres). It is because of this that a lifting bag requires either the bottom to be open to allow air to escape, or to be fitted with a pressure relief valve capable of discharging the surplus air. Figure 113 shows a typical lifting bag in popular use by divers.

Lifting capacities vary from a few kilograms for a diver's personal lifting bag, taken on every dive, to those capable of lifting several tonnes when used on commercial salvage operations. The shape of the bag is very important as one needs to reduce the risk of air spillage, on ascent, to a minimum. In many lifting operations the ascent is very rapid, and sudden deceleration as the surface is reached often leads to swaying. An incorrectly shaped lifting bag would collapse at this point. It is important that the open end is relatively small and that it tapers outward towards the surface, roughly in the shape

Figure 112 Salvaged World War I Battleship with airlocks fitted

Figure 113 Divers using a lifting bag

of a rounded inverted triangle. This shape prevents air loss and gives maximum stability on the surface, especially when the raised object is being towed by a surface vessel. On the larger bags it is necessary to have a deflation valve, but small ones can be physically 'toppled' in order to vent the air.

Valves, however, are the only way of effecting a controlled deflation. Some lifting bags have valves at intervals up the side, which allows for adjustable lifting capabilities.

Figure 114

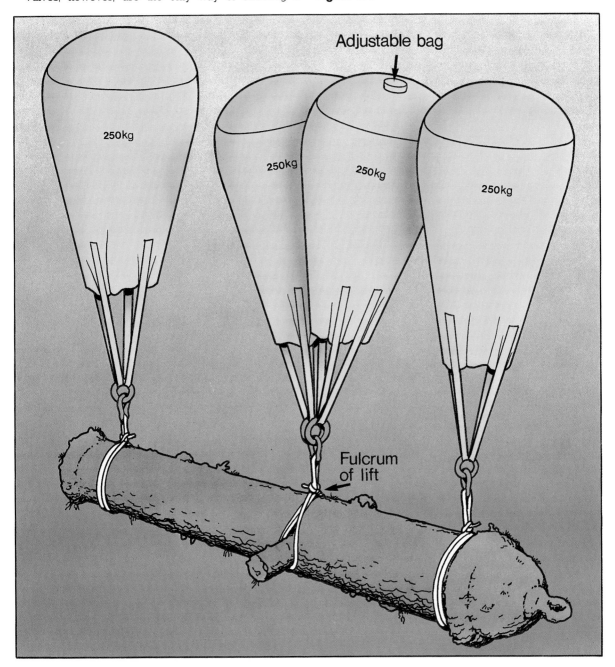

To save cost, some people make their own bags from suitable air-tight material. During stages of manufacture it is important that the fastening strops are sewn on with enough strength to withstand the strain of lifting. A test for this is to fill the lifting bag completely with water on the surface and suspend it from the strops. This represents the amount of strain it will have to repeatedly withstand when full of air. If the strops look insecure, it is realistic to assume they will let you down underwater. Another problem of stitching strops on home-made lifting bags is the prevention of considerable air leakage, through the stitch holes.

In the days before the common availability of lifting bags there were several successful lifting projects using empty oil drums. They were cheap, and when properly lashed together were very effective. The disadvantages were the amount of space they took up, and the extra time taken to fill, compared to lifting bags. Disasters did occur when their lashings gave way, and for these reasons they have been superseded by lifting bags.

While many smaller objects can be raised by fastening the lifting bag directly onto them, many larger objects, for example sunken ships, require the use of wire strops to be positioned in support in order to achieve a balanced lift. The bags are fastened to the strops by the use of shackles, and there are often several bags employed on the same lift. It is very important to simplify underwater operations, and the last thing one needs is to have to tie many knots underwater; many divers have trouble with these on the surface! This has led to the widespread use of shackles and carabiners.

Having calculated roughly the weight of the object you wish to raise, it is better to use several smaller bags rather than one big one. Using multiple bags gives you a greater degree of control, as it may be vital to have a controlled ascent rate on the final lift. Let us assume you calculate the object will require 1000 litres of air in order to lift it. You have the choice of four 250 kilogram bags or one large one capable of lifting 1000 kilograms. When you actually lift the object you find it becomes neutrally buoyant with 800 kilograms of lift. With the large bag there is a danger that you will not be able to control the ascent, once it starts to move. On ascent the air inside will rapidly expand to fill the 'spare' 200 kilogram capability, and unless you have good technique and an easily controllable dump valve an uncontrolled lift will occur. With the four smaller bags, however, you will be able to fully inflate three of them to capacity without the object moving. The fourth bag will be the adjustment device allowing you to feed enough air into it to reach the neutral buoyancy position. The prudent use of a dump valve will allow you to finely tune the ascent, as the other three bags have the same lifting capability for the whole ascent. They will merely vent the excess of expansion. The use of multiple bags has another advantage in that it allows a much more balanced lift. Figure 114 shows an acceptable configuration for using four small bags in the example quoted above. The three full bags are spaced to ensure a balanced lift. It is important for the adjustment bag to be located on the fulcrum of the lift, so an

imbalance is not created. It is often necessary to lower the object to the bottom again in order to re-position one or several of the bags, before you attempt the full lift.

There is no doubt that a successful lifting project is one of the best exercises for engendering interest within a club and to foster links with other clubs. It gives a real sense of purpose to diving. Any project requires a competent leader with a well thought-out dive plan. This should carry built-in flexibility, opportunity for close teamwork and a committed number of divers. Successful lifting projects, when complete, will have given divers experience in underwater searching, buoy laying, boat handling and compressor operation, as well as the skills involved in fitting and filling lifting bags.

Large projects will often involve many different diving clubs. Some years ago the Northern Federation of BSAC branches (Norfed) was involved in a well-publicized project to raise the Loch Doon Spitfire. Nineteen diving clubs from the BSAC and the SSAC were involved in the project. In total, 118 individual divers attended, 109 of whom made 567 dives searching, spending some 373 hours underwater in visibility between zero and 3 metres. Such is the commitment required for a successful project.

Arguably, one of the most successful projects in recent years carried out by amateur divers was the raising of the fishing vessel *Girl Rona* from 55 metres off the coast of Cornwall. What made this a remarkable project were the facts that the *Girl Rona* was raised complete, having sunk mysteriously only a few months before the salvage operation, and the extreme operating depth. The operation also demonstrated the adaptability required when the theoretical plan meets practical difficulties. At the outset it is important to realize that this project was carried out by very experienced divers, operating below the recommended maximum depth limit of 50 metres for air-breathing divers, where decompression and narcosis problems severely restricted diving operations. We highlight it here, however, as a demonstration of a successful ambitious lift, the principles of which could be applied to future projects in shallower water.

The *Girl Rona* was unusual in that the hull and fittings were complete. Most wrecks will be in various stages of decay, and it is likely the project you choose will be to remove objects from it, rather than raise the complete vessel. *Girl Rona* weighed 47 tonnes deadweight, and was quite a new stern trawler when she sank. She lay in an upright position with a list to port. The original plan, because of the extreme depth, was to use two lifting bags, capable of lifting up to 50 tonnes, and to deploy two 30-metre wire strops with eyes at each end. Figure 105 shows the planned lifting method, which was designed to bring the vessel to within 15 metres of the surface, at which point several smaller lifting bags would have been fastened to various strong points on the vessel. Divers would have much more time and better working conditions once *Girl Rona* was suspended at 15 metres. The 30 metre strops would each be shackled to a lifting ring rated at 50 tonnes working load. A further eyed, 25 tonne, 3 metre strop would connect each shackling point to give a trapezium effect. The strops would be held in position by the use of G-clamps and shackles on both the port and starboard rails, to prevent them slipping. Once the vessel had been raised to the surface it was planned to beach her at high water so that pumping out and plugging of holes could be achieved at low water. All strops, shackles, etc., were to be prepared on the surface and lowered down a line attached to the masthead from which they would be manoeuvred into position. A large-volume commercial compressor used for power tools was to be used to inflate the lifting bags.

The project then hit some bad luck with equipment coming loose and, more seriously, the fouling of the salvage boat's anchor in the wreck. This minor disaster effectively put out of action the 30 metre strops as the anchor was fouled in them and could not be released. This point illustrates the need to have alternative methods of attack when undertaking lifting projects. As a way out of the problem, it was decided to attach lifting bags directly onto the hull on the sea bed.

This part of the operation was originally planned for the 15 metre stage. This decision did not mean the end of the problems encountered, as the bags had to be fixed to suitable strong points and evenly distribute their lift. Lifting bags burst to the surface, due to weaknesses on strong points. As a result the first ascent of Girl Rona saw her coming up too fast, the stern reaching the surface before the bows. This allowed the stern bags to collapse and she sank for a second time. Redistribution of bags and still more bag failures followed until eventually she stayed at the surface, in 3 metre waves and a wind gusting to Force 7. She was towed into shallower, calmer water where she was deliberately sent to the sea bed in 15 metres of water. Girl Rona was eventually raised again by positioning lifting bags as low as possible, for maximum lift, and beached in a nearby harbour. She was pumped out, re-fitted and returned to fishing.

The whole project demonstrates the determination and adaptability required to successfully see through any lifting project, and while there are very few amateur projects as ambitious as Girl Rona, one must be prepared for every eventuality.

A few words of warning about such projects. Ensure that it is legal to lift the object, and that once raised it is not going to be left to rust on some beach. Ferrous metal very quickly deteriorates after immersion in salt water once returned to air, and objects are often best left in a stable condition on the sea bed, unless you have the means of metal preservation.

Divers in the UK must also remember that if any payment is received for completed projects, other than for genuine and proven expenses, they are officially classed as being involved in commercial diving operations. This places them under the Health and Safety Executive (HSE) 'Diving Operations at Work Regulations, 1981', where full commercial diving licence requirements are necessary. Involvement in commercial operations, as amateurs, may also invalidate the BSAC third-party insurance.

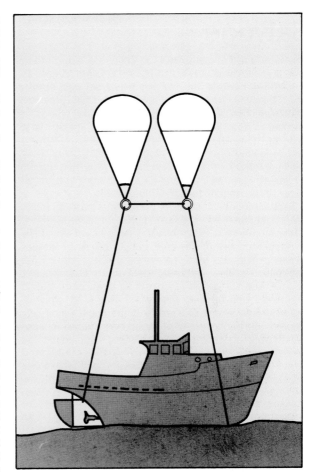

Figure 115/116 Lifting bag configuration used on the 'Girl Rona'

Salvage

The true world of ocean salvage is not the realm of the amateur who dives purely as a hobby. Amateur divers do sometimes become involved in minor salvage operations, for example raising recently sunk small pleasure craft from the sea bed or using small lifting bags to recover a few kilograms of non-ferrous metal. True salvage, however, involves operations like the raising and refloating of complete ships weighing many thousands of tonnes, or raising valuable cargoes from depths which are often well beyond the capabilities and physiology of the standard air-breathing diver.

Large successful salvage operations warrant much media attention and yield large profits for those involved. Many members of the public will have heard about the brilliant recovery of the gold bullion by Keith Jessop/ Wharton Williams from the wreck of the cruiser HMS *Edinburgh* in the depths of the Barents Sea. Equally famous, and an exploit commanding even more public attention, was the vast amount of Nan-King Chinese pottery recovered from a wreck in the South China Sea. The equally public sale of salvaged items raised millions for skipper and owner Mike Hatcher, who found the vessel, and for his backers. For every vastly publicized event, like the two mentioned above, there have been dozens of salvage attempts which created no publicity, and dozens more which brought financial ruin to those involved.

Underwater salvage goes back many years before the invention of the aqualung, although the latter gave the freedom rarely enjoyed by those divers who were burdened by standard diving dress. The primitive diving bell is centuries old, and features in many accounts of successful salvage. The Indian tribes of Florida were for many years highly successful in skindiving to recover gold and silver from the cargoes of treasure galleons sunk along Florida's infamous hurricane coast. The salvage operator of old often risked his life entering the sea in devices made from leather and iron, and often paid the ultimate penalty. Divers today enter the water with the backup of millions of dollars' worth of technical support from full diver-to-surface communications, heated suits, and mixed gas diving capability. Closed-circuit underwater TV and the use of remote-controlled submersibles have given the modern salvor a space-age image. In spite of all this technology, however, the sea is the same potentially cruel, unpredictable environment which can never be underestimated and all salvage operations need an element of luck to succeed.

To be successful a salvage operation needs solid financial backing, and crew who know the job and who can display endurance of exceptional quality. Perhaps above all they need leaders who are engineers with the gift of being able to improvise for the unexpected, and the guts to carry the project through. Throughout salvage history the truly great pioneers have been men who do not let disaster dampen their spirit, but who carry on against all odds with a determination to succeed.

Such an attitude is borne out by the experience of a certain Captain C. E. Hughes-White in World War I, who had already gained a reputation for his relentless determination to succeed and sometimes unorthodox salvage methods. Having just sunk an enemy U-boat by attaching an explosive charge to a wire dragged by minesweepers to cut mine cables, he was summoned before an Admiralty court of inquiry to explain himself. The questioner stated: 'You do not appear to have studied or used any form of attack as laid down by My Lords of the Admiralty?' Hughes-White retorted: 'Good God, no. I used common sense!'

Over the years techniques of salvage have developed, new techniques often being pioneered by men who swore by the adage that 'necessity is the mother of invention'. It is true to say that the last 100 years, with the advent of modern materials and relevant technology, have seen the greatest strides in salvage progress. At one time a mechanical lift was considered to be the most effective means of raising a sunken vessel, the basic technique being to somehow get a bunch of cables around it and strain it to the surface. Then along came tidal lifts, where partially flooded surface lifting craft were attached to the sunken ship at low tide, and as the tide rose water was pumped from the containers. A derivation of this technique was then to attach flooded pontoons to the wreck and to use compressed air to empty them and to raise the wreck using the buoyancy acquired. A legendary figure in ocean salvage, Ernest Cox, then rewrote the rulebook when he pioneered the use of compressed air to raise most of the sunken World War I German High Seas fleet which was scuttled in Scapa Flow in 1919.

All methods are still used, depending on the type of operation being undertaken. A few operations have tried all in an effort to succeed. The last twenty years has seen experiments with polyurethane foams and polystyrene beads as a natural successor to air in raising sunken ships. Polyurethane foam was first used in 1964 to raise a barge off the California coast, the foam forming a rigid cellular material within minutes of being injected. An advantage of the foam over air is the ability it has to seal small openings and ports which do not need to be sealed beforehand, a very time-consuming operation when using compressed air.

One of the inventions which has been used very successfully in archaeological excavations, but has also found a niche in certain salvage operations, is the air-lift. The principle of the air-lift is very simple. A large open-ended vertical pipe is dangled downward and around its lower end on the outside is a compressed air supply, usually from a surface compressor fed by pipe. Some air-lifts have the inside of the chamber perforated with hundreds of tiny holes so that small bubbles of air are released into the pipe, while others have the air supplied direct into the inside of the pipe. The velocity of the rising air, which gives a density of water inside the pipe less than the column of water on the outside, causes water to rush up the pipe. This creates a natural suction on the bottom of the pipe which is ideal for excavation work. Skilled operators can recover delicate objects. The beauty of the system is that it is cheap and very simple. Jacques Cousteau had a version of the air-lift with air supplied from a 200 h.p. compressor capable of lifting 50 tonnes of water per hour, together with 5 tonnes of sand, silt and coral debris. These wastes were sucked up by the hose into metal baskets on the float, having passed through strainers first. A 6-metre lateral length of pipe ensured that debris did not fill the site which had been excavated.

In the salvage world an adaptation of the air-lift principle was successfully employed some years ago to recover nearly 6 million of a 7 million cargo of tins of salmon from the freighter *Diamond Knot*. The value of the salmon was $3.5 million in 1947. Apart from salmon there was additional cargo of herring oil. Two 12-inch suction pipes employed by the divers were tapped into the lowest part of the fish oil tanks. Compressed air pipes were then attached above the level of the oil, and as air was pumped in the oil ran through the suction pipes into barges on the surface. Before the salmon was attempted, $22,000 worth of oil was recovered. Fire-fighting jet pumps were utilized to blast the cans from their cardboard containers. Divers were on the bottom for twenty-four hours as air at 90 p.s.i. was forced through a manifold. Suction hoses raised 4500 litres of water and 800 cans per minute, depositing them in the barge on the surface. After seventy-seven days of work the salvage recovery was $2.1 million. Only 27 per cent of cargo recovered was contaminated with seawater. It is not only gold and silver which are worth diving for.

Figure 117 Salvaged gold ducats

Figure 118 Sunken treasure being winched aboard

Although it was Commodore Frederick Young of the Admiralty Salvage Section who first used compressed air to raise a large vessel when he successfully raised the submarine K-13 in 1917, such exploits are best remembered in Scapa Flow, Orkney, with the work of Ernest Cox and Metal Industries. The complete German High Seas fleet of World War I lay in up to 50 metres of water in the natural harbour of Scapa Flow, having been scuttled in 1919 when it seemed the Armistice negotiations had broken down. Cox bought the 11 battleships, 5 battle cruisers, 8 scout destroyers and 50 regular destroyers, and set up operations at the old Admiralty base at Lyness on the island of Hoy. At the time, official reports stated that no means possible would raise the ships. Cox thought differently. He started his operations by concentrating on the destroyers, which lay in shallower water, by constructing two L-shaped floating docks from one U-shaped dry dock. Each was equipped with pumps, air compressors, engine and boiler rooms with twelve sets of hand-operated winches. Each pulley block was secured to 100-ton tackles bolted to the dock's upright walls. Two men operated each winch handle. The first 750-ton destroyer, V-70, was lifted in 1924, using a mechanical technique of old anchor chains stretched underneath the hull at low tide with the two dock sections taut on either side. During operations the chains snapped, and Cox had to change to lifting cables with flattened centres for the remainder of the operations. Such setbacks were not unusual as the years progressed, and Cox was once described as a mixture of a genius and a mule. By 1925 the team had become so proficient that the average lift time was four days. The men also became so expert with explosives that no one could tell whether a cable had been blasted in half or sawn.

The most spectacular lifts involved the capital ships, which were raised using compressed air. Most of the ships lay upside down or heeled over with their upperworks to the sea bed. Huge airlocks were bolted to the hull by divers to allow workers to descend down a huge 'chimney' to the black and filth of the hull below. All openings had to be sealed both externally and internally. The *Von Moltke* was the first successful lift of a large ship at 23,000 ton lying in 28 metres of water. As the lift started the bow, which was elevated higher than the stern, rose, but a 33-degree list to port occurred. This meant that air inside was 'common', and had been allowed to migrate within the hull due to leaking bulkheads. Bulkheads had to be sealed and airlocks fitted to allow transfer within the hull. Still the list remained, and was only corrected when Cox hung a flooded section of a raised destroyer on the starboard side and inflated the ship's side tanks and bunkers on the port side. During the lift one of the cables was cut by sharp deck edges and the ship's huge weight. Once on the surface her turrets were blown off, as they kept sticking in the mud. She was furnished for the 280-mile tow to the dry dock in Rosyth dockyard on the River Forth, and a kitchen, accommodation and compressors were built on her upturned hull. Unfortunately, as she entered the Pentland Firth a gale blew up and the 6-metre freeboard was soon reduced to 2 metres as air was lost through buffeting.

More confusion heralded her arrival in the Forth, when an argument broke out between two tug skippers as to who was in charge. While this was sorted out the *Von Moltke* narrowly missed one of the supports for the famous Forth railway bridge. She was eventually delivered safe into dry dock, where her hull was stripped and sold for scrap. At the end of Cox's involvement in Scapa Flow, all but 7 of the 74 ships had been raised and salvaged. Today they provide exciting diving for amateurs visiting the Orkney Islands.

It is doubtful that operations of this scale will ever be repeated because of the huge financial commitment. Headline-worthy salvage tends to centre around those events where cargo is valuable, such as the gold in the *Edinburgh* mentioned above. Recent media attention has been centred on the finding of the *Titanic*, and the dramatic pictures relayed by the submersibles used in the search operations. It is unlikely that any salvage will be made on the wreck in the near future due to her extreme depth, the huge investment risk, and the objections from the bereaved. Very few locations, however, can be said to be out of the range of the determined salvor with the aid of modern technology.

Figure 119 (opposite top) WWI German battleship upside down – note compressors to maintain positive buoyancy

Figure 120 (opposite left) WWI battleship being towed

Figure 121 (opposite right) WWI battleship being supported by heavy lifting equipment

Underwater Communications

Reliable underwater communications are an absolute necessity for a safe dive. Communication underwater can be divided into separate areas as follows:

a Visual hand signals
b Line signals
c Simple sound signals including diver recall systems
d Voice communications systems
e Use of lights/strobes

Visual hand signals

The use of visual hand signals is familiar to all divers, and there is no need to go into any detail here regarding the use of standard diver-to-diver underwater signals.

·The use of an international system comes into its own when diving with people who cannot communicate through a common language at the surface. It is incredible how two people who, on the surface, can barely make themselves understood, are immediately able to 'talk' to each other once beneath the surface.

It is well worth considering the possible extension of the standard diver-to-diver visual signals enabling much more in the way of underwater 'conversation'. Diving instructors will be familiar with the range of 'instructional' signals which have been developed and to a large extent standardized. It is relatively easy to tell the students when to watch something being demonstrated and when to perform the drill themselves. Transferred to the open-water situation in normal diving activities, it is possible to devise signals between buddies which add to the standard signals and allow mutual understanding between them. The only limitations are visibility and your imagination.

Another possibility which has been successfully adapted by some divers is the use of deaf and dumb language, which is not difficult to learn in an elementary form.

Many divers carry personal slates, which can be very useful to relay brief messages. Another means of communication underwater is to spell out words in the sand or on any suitable flat object with your finger. Such messages, however, must necessarily be brief and should not be given too quickly.

Line signals

Line signals can be divided into two types: those between diver and diver, and those between diver and surface. The most common use of line signals is between divers engaged in underwater search methods. These searches are covered extensively in 'Specialist Diving'. However, the principles of communication using lines can be established.

The code devised must be easily understood. The BSAC system includes only five separate rope signals. It relies on 'pulls' rather than 'bells', as their interpretation can be confused. A pull is essentially a longer, firmer tug on the line than a bell. Bells are always given in multiples of two. While the system of pulls and bells was well established in the Navy and successfully used, it was mainly deployed when a surface tender was working a solo diver on a diver-to-surface line. The problem for the amateur who is unfamiliar with the system is that one person's pull could be interpreted as another person's bell. Another important principle is to ensure that an important signal is identifiable. Water movement or diver movement is easily confused and mistaken for one pull. More than one pull is usually unmistakable.

Apart from search techniques, mentioned above, divers may well be linked by buddy lines when out of visual contact with each other in poor visibility conditions. It is a simple matter to devise a code of signals which will allow them to communicate along the buddy line.

A surface marker buoy can also be used by the surface party to communicate with the divers if the need arises. The most helpful instruction would be one which required the divers to surface. Alternatively, the SMB could

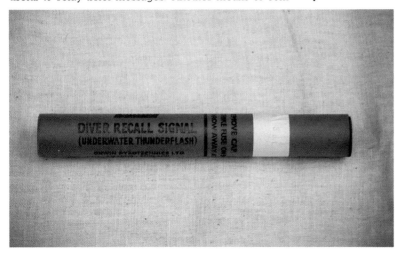

Figure 122 'Thunderflash'

form part of a simple system which allowed the surface cover to direct the divers, for example, if they were systematically searching an area. Signals could be devised to ask the divers to go right or left, stop, go straight on, etc.

Simple sound signals

Sound signals can be used in a similar fashion to line signals. Instead of pulls, messages can be tapped out on the diving cylinder. It is again vital that the code is kept simple and familiar to both divers. Signals must be tapped out very slowly or they will sound continuous. Horns or other audible devices are available for sound communication underwater.

The most common diver recall systems use sound. The thunderflash (see Figure 122) will be familiar to many, and is essentially an underwater firework which is audible. Thunderflashes come in different sizes, and the smaller ones are not always powerful enough. Military diving clubs have access to the Mk 8 thunderflash, which is substantial and very effective. One word of warning about their use. They will only work if submerged, and must be weighted before being set off. Failure to do so only serves to frighten off seagulls. It is important that divers experience hearing a thunderflash underwater, so that they will recognize the sound instantly.

Some years ago a re-usable diver recall system was marketed which used starter pistol blanks and a percussion system activated by water pressure. The cylinder containing the blank was lowered over the side on a length of cord. The sound was clearly audible on the surface, at which point the device was reeled in.

Another diver recall system involving sound uses an outboard motor, which is revved in a recognizable sequence. This method is subject to mistakes in interpretation.

Voice communications systems

Voice communications systems are still very much the domain of the professional diver involved in commercial operations (see Figure 123). Special radio frequencies are said to provide distortion-free reception, a problem with earlier systems.

Communications between diver and diver and between diver and the surface are made possible with such systems. Many divers do not welcome technology which allows voice conversation. For those who require it, however, team efficiency can be greatly enhanced with an effective voice communications system.

Some systems employ a transceiver in the mouthpiece which usually involves wearing a full face mask. The use of older systems requires training in order to speak intelligibly and to understand what is being said underwater, due to the effect of the water on sound. At first there may be a 'Donald Duck' distortion, but with practice this can be overcome.

Use of lights/strobes

Divers frequently become separated, especially in areas of the world with poor underwater visibility. The use of good torches can overcome this problem by helping them stay in contact, the so-called 'Volvo' syndrome. A recent addition to the market is the submersible battery-operated strobe light shown in Figure 124. Designed to fit around the ankles, where they can be seen from either side, strobe lights can, of course, be deployed on other visible parts of the anatomy. Far more powerful than ordinary torches, they must be seriously considered as a safety feature. Visible over great distances, they also provide a very effective marker on the surface and can make the job of searching boats or helicopters much easier.

Figure 123 Underwater telephone system

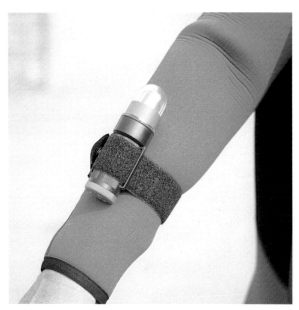

Figure 124 Strobe light

Diver Propulsion Vehicles

A very effective and effortless way for the diver to cover a large underwater area is to use a diver propulsion vehicle, or DPV. They were originally called underwater scooters, as early models were steered by a type of handlebar. They tow a diver through the water at considerable speed and without the need for any strenuous finning.

Essentially, the DPV consists of an electric motor which drives a propeller, and a rechargeable electric battery that supplies energy to the motor. These components are enclosed in a water- and pressure-proof plastic casing with an external switch which controls the power to the propeller. One type of DPV has a two-position switch which enables the diver to select slow speed and long battery life, or high speed and short battery life. Another type of DPV has a variable-pitch propeller which can be adjusted to alter the speed of the vehicle.

There is no steering, as such, built into the DPV. All steering is carried out by the 'driver', who uses his hands, arms and body to turn the vehicle or to point it up or down. With a little initial practice carried out at slow speed, it is possible for the diver/vehicle combination to become very manoeuvrable, and for steering to become accurate.

It should be remembered that a diver in control of such a vehicle is unable to look at wrist-mounted instruments. Most DPVs have a facility for mounting depth gauge and compass on the housing of the vehicle where they can easily be read. However, the diver will have to stop the vehicle occasionally to check the air remaining in his cylinder.

A typical vehicle will tow a diver at up to four knots for a duration of up to one hour – giving a maximum range of some four miles. The battery will need up to ten hours to recharge completely. One company has a quick-change battery-pack which allows a fully recharged battery to be inserted into the vehicle to replace the exhausted power source, thus enabling continued use of the DPV. Having one battery in the unit and at least one on charge is ideal.

The very fact that the DPV is so powerful and able to tow the diver through the water quickly can itself lead to problems. At four knots it is possible for loose equipment to come adrift. Descending rapidly whilst controlling the DPV prevents 'the diver from squeezing his nose for ear clearing. Ascending as rapidly as the DPV is capable will be fraught with the most horrible problems of barotrauma! The DPV is at its best when towing the diver in a straight, horizontal line.

It should be borne in mind that, unless a diving buddy is similarly equipped with a DPV, the diver will be diving alone!

There is no doubt that the DPV is great fun to use. It enables the diver to see more and to go further and, since there is so little effort involved, his air lasts much longer. There is also a serious use for such vehicles. They can be used for surveys and/or searches, enabling a

much larger area to be covered than could be attempted by conventional finning divers. It is doubtful if there is much advantage in using a DPV in conditions of poor visibility, since there is a very real risk of collision. It is exactly like driving a car too fast in fog.

Figure 125 Diver aboard a DPV

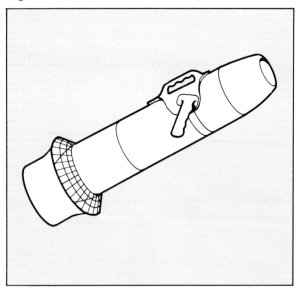

Figure 126 A DPV. All steering is carried out by the diver

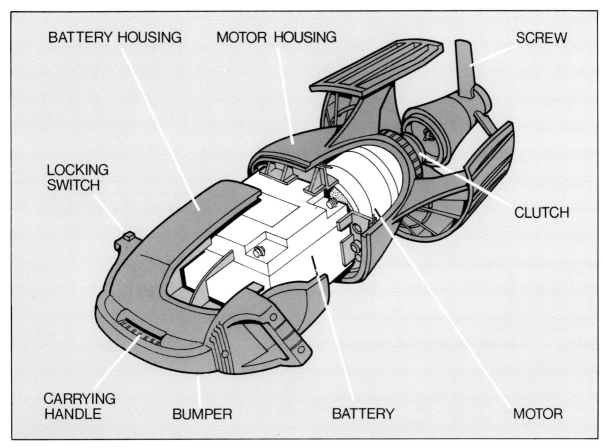

Figure 127 Main features of a DPV

Figure 128 An effortless way to cover large areas

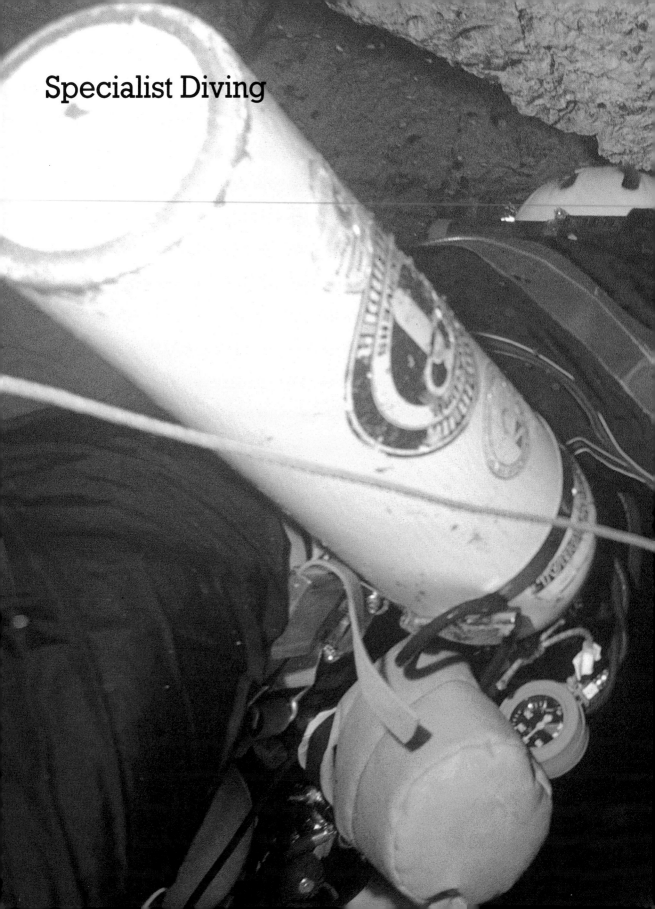

Specialist Diving

Cave Diving

Introduction

Cave, cavern, ice and restricted-surface diving are all categorized as specialist diving, and introduce additional training requirements and potential hazards which the open-water diver generally does not possess nor have to face.

The following sections are an introduction to these specialized subjects and are not intended to provide the reader with the technical means to participate. It must be stressed that even the experienced open-water diver must undergo thorough practical training provided by professional cave diving organizations; cave exploration cannot be learnt from books alone.

Cavers (speleologists) often spend many years caving prior to taking up diving, and are motivated by a desire to explore and extend cave systems. However, many of the techniques developed by cave divers have benefited open-water divers and apply equally to the entering of wrecks, diving under ice, or anywhere access to the surface is restricted.

Cave diving demands a certain philosophy, or attitude of mind, to cope with the additional anxiety created by cold water, darkness, low visibility, claustrophobia and disorientation, which can have disastrous consequences in a cave. However, open-water divers who have already experienced and understand these conditions are perhaps more suited to undertake the additional specialist training required in equipment operation and diving techniques.

Types of caves

Caves fall into several categories.
– Man-made caves, such as old abandoned mine workings and quarries which have filled with water.
– Natural springs (underground rivers that usually flow to the surface).
– Sinkholes, caused by rainwater seeping through cracks in limestone rock, which gradually dissolves. Over a period of time large chasms are created which become deeper, wider and longer. Eventually, these chasms become so large that the water is no longer able to support the surrounding rock and the roofs of the chambers collapse inwards. The chambers continue to collapse until the cavern breaks through to the surface. Sinkholes do not have a run of water, but they may have a flow; this is the point where the water moves into the sinkhole and a 'siphon' at the point where it moves out. (See Figure 130.)

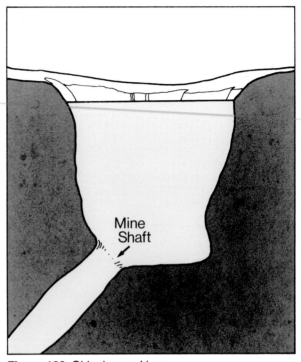

Figure 129 Old mine workings

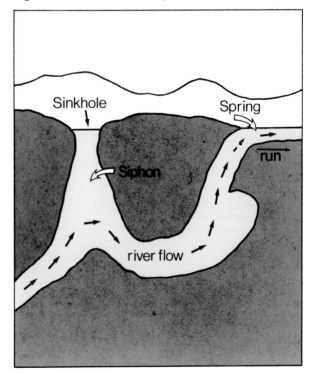

Figure 130 Sinkhole and spring

Visibility

Although most caves contain crystal-clear water, they are dark and gloomy. The floors are usually covered with rocks and a fine sediment or silt caused by soil falling in when the cavern was formed. When disturbed sediment can very quickly reduce visibility to zero; to try to prevent this a cave diver should adopt the bent-leg finning action. (See Figure 131.) By finning close to the cave roof, the diver can avoid disturbing the sediment although exhaled air from his regulator may still dislodge mud and silt which has accumulated on ledges. Poor visibility can also be experienced when the diver passes through a boundary between two layers, fresh and salt (halocline), or in the shallower regions where the water tends to be warmer and the growth of algae reduces light penetration. Sunkholes are sometimes strewn with debris – discarded vehicles, trees which, due to erosion of the bank, have fallen in, and in the case of old mine workings, machinery. All of these items are potentially dangerous in poor or zero visibility.

The largest single cause of cave diving accidents is the lack of a continuous guideline to the surface. Guidelines for cave systems which are relatively free from silt are usually made of thin nylon (plastic line will float and tangle easily). However, thicker floating line is used when there is a risk of the line being buried by silt, as its removal can reduce visibility for some distance ahead. The guideline, which is normally wound from a reel, is belayed at regular intervals with lead weights or tied around boulders on the cave floor. It is tagged with light-coloured plastic tape denoting distance or direction. (See Figure 132.) As the name implies, the lines are used for guidance purposes, and should not be used by the diver to pull himself along through cave systems. In some popular caves more permanent lines of different colours are laid to indicate direction and distance. (See Figure 133.)

Cave divers always follow the 'one-third rule' of air consumption. The diver uses one-third of his air going into the cave, reserving one-third for his return and the final third for emergencies. Clearly, the amount of air available is important. Cave divers will always carry large enough air cylinders to complete the planned dive safely, even to the extent of carrying more than two cylinders if required.

Figure 131 A cave diver following a guide line – note bent leg action

Figure 132 Cave diver laying dive line in poor visibility – note knife and instruments on forearm

Figure 133 Following a line – note the helmet torches

Equipment

In cave diving, every piece of equipment has at least one back-up. A minimum of two cylinders are carried by the diver. Both are rigged with separate regulators (not connected to a manifold), and preferably with DIN-threaded valves (A clamps are prone to accidental damage in confined areas). Hoses should be colour-coded so that the high-pressure gauge can be easily identified. The regulators should be mounted so that the hoses come in from either side of the diver to avoid confusion. Each regulator should be fitted with a neck strap so that they are instantly available when changing from one cylinder to another, or if the regulator is accidentally dislodged from the diver's mouth. (See Figure 135.) British cave divers usually prefer side-mounted cylinders so that the diver can manoeuvre them through narrow low-roofed sections or locations where there are known to be confined or narrow passages. Side-mounted cylinders also enable the diver to deal with any regulator or line entanglement problems which occur within his sphere of vision. (See Figure 135.)

A minimum of three underwater torches are required for cave diving; however, it is recommended that a reliable fourth torch is also carried. Torches are usually mounted either side of a helmet, which has holes drilled in the top to allow the diver's exhaled air to escape. This system has the advantage of freeing the hands and protecting the head from injury. (See Figure 134.)

Pressure gauges, depth gauge, watch, compass and knife are usually located on the diver's arms for easy reading and access. This also reduces the risk of the equipment snagging on unseen obstructions.

Figure 135 Cave diver with side-mounted cylinders, helmet lights and line reel

Figure 134 Cave diver with back-mounted cylinders, each separately valved

Figure 136 British cave diving harness, with cylinders set for side-mounting

Neutral buoyancy for the cave diver is critical if he is to avoid stirring up silt, thereby reducing visibility. Buoyancy adjustment for the cave diver wearing a wet suit is normally achieved by using the lifejacket direct-feed system only. Cave divers prefer not to fit emergency air cylinders or CO_2 cartridges as there is a risk of accidentally inflating the lifejacket, which would result in the diver being pinned to the roof of the cave. With this problem in mind, cave divers prefer to wear a more firmly secured weightbelt, rather than the standard quick-release type used in sport diving. For cold water conditions a dry suit is essential. However, unlike the wet-suited diver, buoyancy adjustment is achieved by suit inflation, and a lifejacket is considered unnecessary.

Although the buddy system is considered fundamental for sport diving safety it is not always possible, or desirable, in some cave diving situations, particularly those cave systems found in the British Isles which tend to be very constricted. Because of the restricted nature of some cave systems, it would be impracticable to have two divers in very close proximity as this could increase the risk of entanglement and confusion in poor or zero visibility. Cave diving techniques differ in other parts of the world. Some of the larger cave passages currently being explored on the continents of Australia and America use the buddy system extensively, but still place much more emphasis and reliance on their equipment back-up systems and safety procedures than is common for sport divers. For this reason, specialist training with a professional cave diving organization should be sought.

Figure 137 Wearing side-mounted cylinders, a diver negotiates an underground canyon

Figure 138 Two divers with independently-valved back-mounted cylinders prepare to dive an underwater cave

Cold-water Diving

Winter diving and summer diving cannot be treated in the same way, since the effects of cold water and the atmospheric temperature, both on the diver's body and his diving equipment, bring an additional set of problems.

The causes and effects of hypothermia on the diver are explained in *Sport Diving* (pp. 90–3). However, it is worth remembering that cold slowly robs the diver of his ability to react efficiently. It is always potentially dangerous, and it is essential that divers minimize the effects of cold, both on their body and on their equipment.

Effects of cold water on equipment
The risk of regulator freezing begins to be significant as the water temperature reaches 5°C, but many other factors also play a part. The more recent two-stage regulator works as follows. At each stage the reduction in pressure is accompanied by a drop in the temperature of the air, this temperature drop being influenced by the size of the pressure reduction and the rate of the flow of air. Modern high performance regulators with higher cylinder pressures can be more prone to freezing problems. More air delivered in a shorter time will create larger temperature drops in the first stage. Higher intermediate pressures coupled with greater flow rates will also increase the temperature drop in the second stage.

Figure 140 Ice forming on the first stage

Figure 139 Avoid the second stage being submerged in cold conditions

Figure 141 Second stage 'free flowing'

Insulated first stages

The problem of ice forming within the first stage where the first drop in pressure occurs, inhibiting the movement of the reduction mechanism, has effectively been solved by the provision of an oil-filled chamber which insulates the mechanism from the water. (See Figure 142.) The formation of ice before the first stage indicates that the water has been cooled by the first-stage body, but does not necessarily indicate that it is not working correctly.

The cooled air from the first stage passes along the medium-pressure hose and is influenced by the ambient water temperature. At the second stage the further reduction in pressure is accompanied by another drop in temperature. Apart from the fact that this air is cold to breathe, and will eventually affect the diver's body temperature, there is no real problem until this cooled air meets water or water vapour.

One source of water is that introduced by the diver while swimming at the surface, taking his regulator out to talk, or allowing his second stage to become flooded prior to submerging. All these actions should be avoided. The second source of water is from the diver's exhaled air. This is difficult to avoid in a single-hose regulator. The incoming cold air cools the mechanism, causing moisture to condense on it. This moisture is soon frozen, and a build-up of ice can occur. If this ice forms in a position which can inhibit the operation of the inlet valve then it may become blocked, usually in the open position, and a free flow of air will result.

At this point the temperature in the second stage is below the ambient water temperature. If the regulator is removed from the mouth and flooded, its temperature will eventually rise and the ice may be thawed. Meanwhile, the diver will need something from which to breathe. If he is wearing an Octopus with a protected first stage, he should be able to use this since it has not suffered the effects of flow-induced cooling. However, this solution will suffer from a wet second stage, and it is reasonable to anticipate the onset of freezing after a similar period of time.

If the surface temperature is extremely low (−5°C to −30°C), then breathing through the regulator on the surface will be sufficient to form ice, due to the instant freezing of the moisture in the diver's exhaled breath. In this situation check regulator functioning *before* exposing it to the cold. Before the dive take no more than one breath from the regulator before submerging.

The dryness of the air in the cylinder has little effect. If the water vapour content of the air is relatively high, when the cylinder is immersed in cold water the air is cooled below its dew point and the excess water vapour is released as condensation on the inner walls. This creates a problem of internal condensation which will contribute to internal corrosion.

In water temperature below 6°C divers should be prepared for regulator freezing. If you plan to dive in these conditions try to keep the inside of the second stage as dry as possible, and use a regulator which has an insulated first stage. Try to exert the minimum of energy, since increased effort requires deeper breathing, which in turn increases the flow through the regulator, producing an increased drop in the air temperature. Divers should understand that cold-water diving involves additional risks, and should prepare accordingly.

Figure 142 Oil-filled first stage

Ice Diving

In many respects ice diving is similar to cave diving, in that the diver's safe return to the surface is generally reliant on his ability to exit through the entry point. Apart from the fact that it is usually very much colder (although visibility is generally good under ice) the ice diver's equipment will resemble in many ways that which is required by the cave diver. Ropes, safety lines, and torches are just as important!

Because of the risks inherent in diving under ice, divers should only undertake dives where the ice is a single, solid, and stationary sheet. Before venturing onto the ice, make sure it will stand the weight of the surface party, divers and equipment. For safety, the surface party should be wearing lifejackets, wet suits or dry suits – in case the ice gives way! Tools will be required to cut a hole in the ice. Ice axes and augers are the most suitable. The hole should be at least 2 metres in width and the hole should be marked underneath with a flashing strobe beacon to facilitate easy location by the returning divers.

Safety lines

Dives should be conducted with one diver in the water at a time, and with the diver attached to a separate lifeline and controlled by an experienced tender on the surface. The lifeline should be securely attached to the diver with a bowline knot round the chest, under all other equipment. The end of the lifeline should then be securely fastened to a fixed or stationary object, preferably ashore. In addition to the line tender, there should be a stand-by diver fully equipped and ready to enter the water with an additional safety line twice as long as that being used by the diver. There should never be more than one diver under the ice at any one time to avoid the possibility of the lifelines becoming entangled.

Should a diver become separated from his lifeline he should surface slowly and remain stationary under the ice to conserve air. A diver trapped under ice will find it is virtually impossible to cut through with a diving knife. This is because he has very little purchase; the more he forces against the ice, the more he is forced down. Even if he is equipped with an axe he is unlikely to make much of an impression. In the event of a lost diver, the stand-by diver should enter the water and commence a circular sweep under the surface of the ice at the full extent of his lifeline, gradually reducing his circular search until the diver is located. Both can return along the lifeline. If, however, this proves unsuccessful, the same search technique should be carried out on the bottom.

As with cave diving, a minimum of two separate cylinders should be used. Both cylinders should be fitted with separate regulators with insulated first stages. Dry suits are essential for this type of diving.

Figure 143 Divers prepare for an ice dive by cutting a hole in the ice

Figure 144 The Prince of Wales dives under polar ice

Figure 145

Restricted-surface Diving

If a diver enters a wreck or cavern during the course of a dive leaving no clear route to the surface, then this must be considered restricted-surface diving.

Cavern diving

Exploring underwater caverns can be an exciting experience, particularly in tropical waters. Cavern roofs are often decorated with a variety of sponges, corals and marine life, some of which only flourish in the darkness offered by these underwater sanctuaries.

Before entering any cavern you should first check that the entrance is large enough. Shine your torch through the opening and try to assess the internal size of the cavern. If the cavern is judged too small for two divers to enter safely, then it is probably not worth taking the risk. However, if you have prepared for this eventuality, it may be acceptable for your buddy to remain at the entrance of the cavern and act as a tender using a reel and line. Make sure all your hoses and gauges are stowed securely and not dangling, otherwise your progress through the entrance may come to an abrupt halt.

Once inside, orientate yourself with the entry point, and finely adjust your buoyancy so that you can keep clear of the cavern floor. Try to keep your finning to a minimum otherwise visibility will soon deteriorate. Apart from the safety aspects, carrying a torch is essential if you are to appreciate the true colours within. Remember, any cavern more than a few metres in length should be approached with all the caution surrounding a cave dive.

Figure 146 Divers entering an underwater cavern

Entering wrecks

For the diver who only wishes to explore superficially the external structures of wrecks, there are a number of potentially dangerous situations to consider.

Descending a shotline in poor visibility towards an unseen wreck is usually enough to concentrate most divers' minds, but reaching the bottom and finding oneself virtually surrounded by rusting steel is a situation most divers do not expect. Nevertheless it can happen! Shotlines can find their way through cargo holds and penetrate deep inside wrecks. Presented with this situation you should avoid letting go of the shotline until your eyes have become accustomed to the darkness, and you can orientate yourself with your surroundings. Your arrival may well have stirred up the visibility. Should this improve, it is still worth using your reel as a guideline by attaching the free end to the shotline before proceeding to explore your immediate surroundings. If

the visibility remains bad, then abandon the dive and return to the surface via the shotline. A more detailed examination of wreck penetration can be found in 'Wreck Diving', pp. 50–79.

Swimming through sections of open wreckage can be irresistible to most divers. However, it must be remembered that wrecks are generally unstable both in terms of their deteriorating structure and their position relative to the sea bed. Rusting metal which is disturbed by a passing diver can suddenly collapse, blocking exits or possibly causing injury.

Always proceed with caution. Check that there is sufficient space for you to negotiate the passage without disturbing any silt or metal. If in doubt, swim to the other end and check your exit before entering. Wrecks nearly always have sharp edges which can inflict deep cuts, even when gloves are worn.

Divers are often tempted to enter a wreck on the spur

Figure 147 A diver exploring a wreck

of the moment, without considering the consequences. Unless you are experienced and familiar with the structure and condition of a wreck, the casual wreck diver should avoid the temptation to enter open doorways and holes where there is no indication of an exit.

Gill and tangle nets

There are a number of other unforeseen hazards which may restrict a diver's ascent to the surface. Wrecks have always captured the nets of trawlers, and many are covered with lost equipment of this nature. But it is only in recent years that the deliberate netting of wrecks has become commercially viable.

Gill nets and tangle nets are usually deployed on or near wrecks where fish tend to congregate. However, they often break free from their moorings, and either tumble endlessly along the sea bed or cocoon themselves around the wrecks. Made from mono- or multi-filament line, the nets are difficult to see in good visibility. In poor visibility, the diver has little chance of detecting their presence until he is brought to a halt and entangled.

A typical diver's knife is virtually useless for cutting mono-filament line. Surgical scissors or specially designed line cutters are the most effective tools for this situation. Both these implements should be attached to the diver's arms, where they are easily accessible. (See Figure 149.) Clearly, if you dive regularly on wrecks where nets are likely to be found, then it is a sensible precaution to equip yourself with these accessories. Should you find yourself entangled, do not struggle as this often worsens the situation. Try to gain a little positive buoyancy in order to tension the netting before attempting to cut it.

Figure 148 Lights are useful accessories on deep wrecks

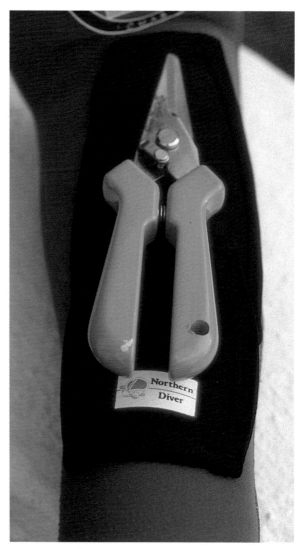

Figure 149 Cutting tool and pocket

Deep Diving

In the days of thin wet suits, lower-capacity cylinders, and less efficient regulators the problems of diving deep were not so significant as today. Large-capacity cylinders, highly efficient regulators and thermally efficient wet and dry suits have led to many divers venturing regularly to depths which some years ago would have been considered the limit.

The absolute limit recommended for amateur divers is 50 metres. In the waters which surround the British Isles, and similar diving environments around the world, such a depth will always be a challenge because of visibility, lack of natural light and low temperature. In other parts of the world with clear tropical water, diving to such a depth may be regarded as routine. Regardless of these differences, dives to such depths need very careful planning as the body undergoes the same physiological changes with regard to decompression sickness, narcosis, etc.

The BSAC diving manual *Sport Diving* outlines all the extra risks involved in deep diving as well as defining what a deep dive is, split into various categories. Also covered are considerations regarding air consumption and calculation, personal equipment, buoyancy, and boat support. This section will expand on the above, giving practical advice on stage decompression diving, including techniques for static and moving water.

The BSAC '88 decompression tables have been computed after bringing together all current knowledge of how nitrogen is eliminated after a dive. One of the changes of philosophy which they introduce is the conclusion that decompression stops are good for you. A dive with a controlled ascent which includes stops is now considered to be part of a safe decompression process. The surface interval between dives is a stop within this procedure. It is especially important, therefore, that provision for accurate and safe decompression stops is built into all dives, not only those below 30 metres.

What type of extra equipment will we need for dives involving decompression stops?

1 A minimum shot weight of 25 kilograms. An alternative could be a grappling anchor. The shotline needs to have a minimum diameter of 15 millimetres, and must be supported at the surface by a large buoy (e.g., 1 metre circular Dan).

2 A 'lazy' shot and line with large loops marked at 9 and 6 metres for stage decompression. A lazy shot is one suspended from the surface to mid-water, the weight usually being about 5 metres below the first stop. A diver's ability to conduct and accurately maintain stops in, for example, a rough sea or tidal stream is made more practical when using a lazy shot.

3 Two full cylinders with regulators fitted, and checked to be suitably fastened, to the loops of the lazy shot at 9 and 6 metres. Each cylinder should be fitted with two second stages (Octopus rig). It must be stressed that these must only be used if the divers have insufficient air

to complete a decompression schedule, and should not be considered as part of their planned air capacity.

4 When the dive planned involves stage decompression, it is essential that the divers find their way back to the shotline. A fail-safe way of doing this, in poor visibility, is to use distance lines clipped to the base of the shotline. These can then be reeled out as the diver swims away from the shot and, if they are marked with regular distance markers, for example every 5 metres, can be a useful aid. Care must be taken against entanglement around the legs and fin straps, and their use is best practised in shallower conditions with better visibility. If visibility is good and the divers know the site, then such distance lines are less important. In certain situations, for example on drop-offs, walls, tunnels and gullies, this system is inoperable.

5 An 'up-line' with weighted snap clips or carabiners at either end to connect the main shotline to the lazy shot.

Figure 150 shows the deployment of the above list of equipment in a non-tidal situation. Moving water would need certain adaptations. These techniques are described below.

Successful deep diving depends on thorough organization and detailed planning. This involves competent dive leaders, the use of charts, tide tables, and local information to plan the best time to dive a site and to estimate accurately the water depth over the selected site. The boat used must be suitable for the number of divers involved and the extra equipment needed. Decompression stops must be planned before the dive and noted on a slate carried by the diver. The Dive Planning and Recording Worksheet in the BSAC '88 tables is designed for this purpose.

Figure 150 Deployment of equipment for a deep dive in non-tidal water

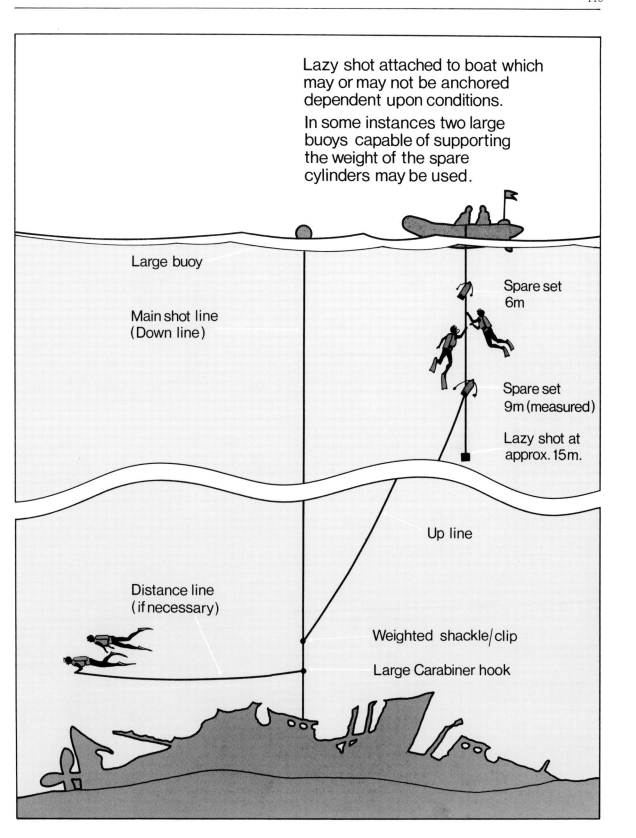

Lazy shot attached to boat which may or may not be anchored dependent upon conditions.

In some instances two large buoys capable of supporting the weight of the spare cylinders may be used.

Large buoy

Main shot line (Down line)

Spare set 6m

Spare set 9m (measured)

Lazy shot at approx. 15m.

Up line

Distance line (if necessary)

Weighted shackle/clip

Large Carabiner hook

Decompressing in moving water

Before diving in waters with strong tidal streams you must consider carefully how long you may realistically spend decompressing. The BSAC '88 tables allow a maximum of twenty-one minutes of stage decompression. Planning for such extremes involves consideration of cold, discomfort in heavy swells, and the possibility of increasing tidal streams. To be extended like a flag on a windy day on a shotline is very uncomfortable and should be avoided. A small 'tidal window' may mean that it is unavoidable that the last pair of divers have to decompress when the tide has begun to flow. If this situation occurs, the plan may allow for the divers to unclip the lazy shot from the main shot, with the former being suspended from the boat. The boat then drifts with the divers, who are thus not affected by the tidal stream. This technique may well pose problems of manoeuvrability if the boat is operating in a busy channel or on a lee shore, and must be used with extreme caution. It may be prudent to suspend the lazy shot from a large buoy(s) capable of supporting the weight and thus allowing the boat to stay mobile.

Drift diving in deep moving water requires special techniques and careful planning and must only involve one pair of divers submerged at any time from each boat. Manoeuvrable boats, such as RIBs or inflatables, are best suited to this type of operation for reasons which become obvious when one appraises the techniques involved.

Each diving pair must be marked with a larger than normal surface marker buoy. Immediately prior to the divers ascending, the boat crew attach a previously prepared lazy shot to the SMB using a carabiner or snap hook. The system is lowered to the required depth and the ascending divers carry out their required decompression schedule with a covering boat following them. Again, great care must be taken about the choice of site for the reasons listed above.

To avoid trailing SMBs over sites where divers are likely to remain reasonably static, for example, a wreck site, the use of a 'delayed SMB' should be considered. Each pair of divers carries a special inflatable SMB with 10 metres of cord attached. Figure 151 shows its configuration. Once inflated, the buoy assumes a tube about 10–15 centimetres in diameter and 1 metre high. Made in yellow, orange or red heavy-duty rip-stop nylon material, it is easily visible. As the divers ascend to their first stop at 9 metres, they should hold the buoy and allow the weighted bobbin to sink. The buoy is inflated with air and allowed to surface. The divers then hold onto the end of the line and carry out decompression. This device is particularly useful if divers fail to find their way back to the shotline to decompress. They can then ascend, and their position can be noted whilst they carry out stage decompression. They will not have the benefit of the emergency air supply, however, and this is another reason why all ascents should be timed to give enough air for the decompression schedule.

Mid-water decompression stops, without the aid of a shotline, rely on divers' careful buoyancy control and ease of mind in coping with mid-water conditions.

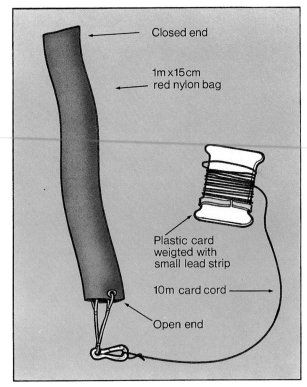

Figure 151 Delayed SMB

Figure 152 Divers using SMB in moving water

Diving with a 'waster'

A group of experienced deep wreck divers in the UK have developed an interesting and effective alternative technique over many years of diving on wrecks over 40 metres in slack water conditions. This involves the use of a diver-to-surface line carried by each pair of divers. The end of the main line is tied off, leaving behind an extra 3 metre length of thinner line as a sacrificial 'waster' when the dive is completed. Each pair of divers has a surface tender who pays out the line as the divers descend and move around on the bottom. Because of the depths involved and the fact that wreck sites are fairly compact, there is never any extreme lateral movement away from the boat. At the end of a predetermined time the divers will tie off the waster onto a suitable piece of wreckage and ascend up the main line. At the same time, the surface tender ties off the line to give a firm rope on which to decompress. The number of pairs which can successfully be deployed depends on the size of the boat. Care needs to be taken that the different lines do not cross in the water, and that the boat does not drift off site and snap the wasters prematurely. Once the divers are out of the water, the main line can be tensioned to break the waster on the sea bed. If slack water time permits, a second pair of divers could descend down the first pair's line and carry on from where the latter left off.

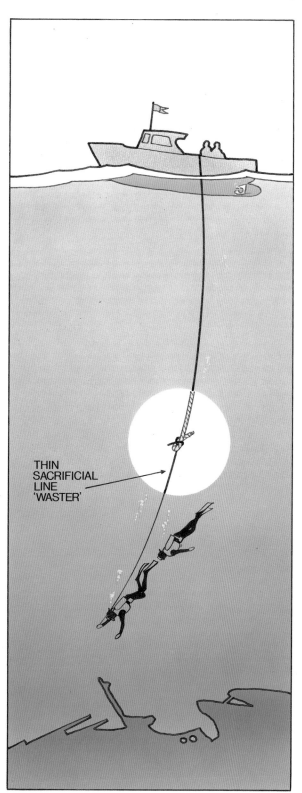

THIN SACRIFICIAL LINE 'WASTER'

Figure 153 Divers returning via the anchor line

Figure 154 Diving with a waster

Drift Diving

Most diving is planned for a period when the in-water conditions are as quiet as possible. When diving in tidal waters, divers will take the trouble to work out the time at which slack water is expected on any particular day. Diving during a period of slack water gives the divers the most suitable conditions for moving freely about the bottom.

At some dive sites slack water is unpredictable, and at others there may simply be no slack water at all – the tide or current changes speed or direction but can never really be called 'slack'. Since it is very tiring for a diver to swim against even a moderate current for anything other than a very short time, and if the area is sufficiently interesting, consideration might be given to *drift diving*.

Drift diving can be simply described as diving in a tidal stream or current and allowing the stream or current to carry the diver along. It can be quite an exhilarating experience, moving through the water at speed without needing to swim except during the descent and ascent.

To ensure safety it is essential that there is constant contact between the divers and the surface – the two divers should be roped together and have a strong line or rope running from them to the surface. The surface end of the line should be attached to a large surface marker buoy. This must be of sufficient buoyancy to ensure that it cannot be pulled under the surface by the combined effort of the two divers and the current – a minimum of about 30 kilograms.

A conventional reel and line can be used, provided it is sufficiently strong to stand the drag of two divers against a current. Many drift divers prefer to use a length of strong rope, about one and a half times the maximum depth to be encountered.

The surface marker buoy is kept in sight by the surface boat cover, which *must* be under power and keep station with the buoy at all times. The divers, the marker buoy, and the boat will all be subject to the current but not necessarily to the same extent. The current on the sea bottom may differ from that on the surface. The marker buoy and the boat will also be affected by any wind. All of these factors must be appreciated by the boatman in order to maintain station in an appropriate position for recovering the divers safely at the end of the dive.

If the divers are using a rope, rather than a reel and line, it is probable that they will surface directly, without winding in or coiling the rope. In this case, they will surface some distance away from the surface marker buoy – another factor to be considered by the boatman.

No more than two pairs of divers should be allowed into the water at the same time. To make recovery easier, stagger their entries so that they surface at different intervals.

Figure 155 Drifting using a surface marker buoy

Underwater Work

Underwater work is more the domain of the professional diver, who will be trained and equipped to carry out specific or general tasks depending on the area or industry in which he is employed. The oil industry employs a large number of divers, who are involved in the fitting, maintenance and inspection of equipment and plant. Other diving companies will specialize in underwater clearance in harbours and rivers, or in salvage operations. The aim of this section is not to outline details of the above, but to give guidance on the type of underwater tasks which come within the possibilities of the amateur diver without the backup of a full commercial organization.

Sport Diving outlined some simple tasks which divers frequently become involved in. These included measurement, net/rope removal, recovery of lobster/ crab pots and simple surveying techniques. What other tasks do amateur divers frequently become engaged in?

Wreck diving undoubtedly opens up many opportunities, and many thousands of divers throughout the world spend all their underwater time so involved. Removing artefacts from wrecks is common practice, although in some parts of the world, for example Truk Lagoon, this is forbidden. The sunken Japanese fleet there remains undisturbed and are for eyes and cameras only. It is important that divers fully understand the legality of such activities. However, due to the restrictive and unprofitable nature of most salvage laws, much illegal removal of artefacts goes on. Most divers are only interested in collecting souvenirs, and never go wreck diving in order to make money. Portholes, telegraphs, deck lights, etc., are often mounted on displays and make very attractive fittings. (See Figure 157.)

The following passages concentrate on the art of porthole removal, but many of the principles involved relate to most tasks of underwater work on wrecks.

Brass portholes are present on nearly all ships, although some have steel ones. The German light cruisers which were scuttled in Scapa Flow all have the latter. Passenger-carrying vessels have the greatest number of portholes, which are usually restricted to accommodation/eating areas. Many cargo vessels have portholes only in the stern or bows accommodation areas, the middle sections being rather barren.

How, then, are portholes removed, once located? A standard porthole above the vessel's waterline has three components. (See Figure 158.) The opening 'light', with glass, hinges on a backing plate which is usually bolted onto the steel hull. The rounded boltheads are flush to the outside of the hull with the nuts on the inside. The glass may well be intact, unless explosions through sinking or past salvage attempts have blown it out. The final component is a storm cover which clamps down over the glass light in bad weather conditions.

Porthole glass is about 2 centimetres thick, yet such is the power of the sea that, following a storm some years ago, a crew member found shards of shattered glass

Figure 156 Ship's bell

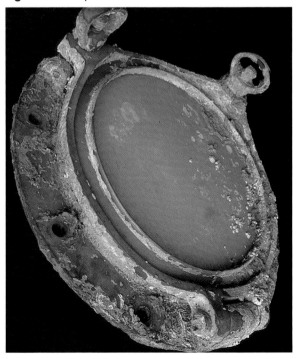

Figure 157 A ship's porthole before being cleaned

embedded in his pillow from a porthole where he had neglected to fasten down the storm cover. Not all portholes open, however. Some, near the waterline, have the glass mounted in the backing plate. In most portholes the backing plate and the opening light are made of brass, while the storm cover is steel. The opening light hinges on a brass pin and can be easily removed by using a suitable chisel, drift and a hammer. It is often necessary to angle the chisel under the top of the pin in order to start it to move, having first hit the bottom of the pin two or three times to lift it proud of the hinge. Once it begins to move, the drift is used to push it completely clear of the hinge. Some divers only remove the opening light, but to do so effectively spoils the find. A little time and effort can remove the whole lot, although this may mean the removal of up to twelve nuts. A sharp cold chisel and a lump hammer are usually all one needs, as most porthole nuts/bolts are steel and are in varying states of decay. Some divers carry adjustable spanners, but these are often unnecessary. It is important to realize that portholes can only be removed once access to the *inside* of the hull has been made possible. Many a wreck has rows of tantalizing portholes which divers can only inspect from the outside.

Figure 159 A port hand lamp

Figure 158 A ship's porthole after cleaning

Figure 160 Ship's propellor – made of steel!

Once inside the area where you will work, you will often find space very restricted and darkness to be a problem. Any underwater work of this nature will produce in-water sediment, which will further restrict visibility. Tools that are carelessly placed on the floor can easily fall into nooks and crannies and be impossible to find again. Important tools are best secured with a lanyard to prevent this happening. Some divers enter the water with a purpose-built tool belt, which has a dual role of weightbelt. Illumination can be a problem as both hands will be needed. There are two solutions to this problem. Where space allows have one's buddy shine the torch in the appropriate place. Where space does not allow this, or where the buddy is otherwise engaged, fasten the torch on some appropriate part of the body. This is only possible with slim pencil-beamed torches, which are readily available, but it is very effective. Some divers strap their torch to the arm of the hand used for holding the chisel. Those wearing wet suits can even tuck it up the sleeve to give the same effect. This keeps both hands free, and is a means of easily directing the light. Another similar method involves the use of a caving-type plastic helmet which has torch-mounting brackets attached. These direct the light in whichever direction the diver happens to be looking. A similar effect can be achieved by tucking the lit torch into a wet hood, if worn.

Removing porthole nuts can be remarkably easy. Before attempting to unscrew them it is worthwhile giving each nut two or three blows with a lump hammer. This action jars away any debris, and is often sufficient to loosen badly decayed nuts so that they can be hand turned. If they will not turn by hand it will be necessary to chisel them loose. Nuts and bolts were designed to be turned, and it is better to place a sharp cold chisel at sufficient an angle against one of the accessible nut 'flats' and strike in an anti-clockwise direction. Most nuts will succumb to this treatment and start to turn. If this fails it may be necessary to split the nut using the chisel, but this time angling it across the face. The ease of this operation depends on the condition of the nuts. Don't be tempted to use too heavy a hammer as repeated striking will lead to painful wrists. For ease of access to the nuts it will often be simpler to remove the opening light with a chisel and drift first of all, as outlined above. It can easily be reassembled on the surface.

Occasionally one finds that a different fixing method other than steel nuts and bolts has been used. It is not uncommon to find steel rivets, which prove very difficult to remove. If it is possible to saw one of the rivet heads off they can sometimes be drifted out. Unfortunately, sawing will invariably lead to unsightly marks on the brass which are very difficult to remove. With care the rivets could be removed using a hand drill, but this method will be very time consuming. The most difficult of all encountered involves countersunk brass screws flush to the outside of the hull. Drilling would be the only effective way of removing these.

Any underwater work involving hammering or levering is very difficult unless one can wedge oneself against something solid. The effectively weightless environment means that if the diver tries to push against anything, he will lift himself rather than the object, unless supported as outlined. It is usually no problem when removing a porthole, as there are many convenient bulkheads for this purpose.

It is very important that correct safety procedures are followed when entering a wreck, and that 'brass fever' does not overtake reasoning. No piece of metal is worth losing a life for, although several divers have died in this fashion over the years. One cannot stress enough the need to be methodical and to carefully monitor dive time and air supply. When working, air consumption can easily double or even treble normal figures and this must be taken into account. Underwater work is one of the adjustment factors to be borne in mind when calculating decompression requirements.

Divers may well be advised to work in pairs, taking it in turns to rest. The resting diver should keep a careful watch on time and air supply. This is easy when contents gauges are used, but if divers are using air reserve systems they must abandon operations once a reserve has been pulled.

Once the object removed is free from the wreck, it is vital that divers do not try to swim it to the surface. Divers have died doing this. Personal lifting bags with about 25-kilogram capacity are adequate for many items and should be carried if you plan to lift small objects. An alternative method is to take a reel with a line of reasonable breaking strain and tie it off on the bottom, unwinding the reel while surfacing. Once on the boat it can be hand- or winch-lifted. One will occasionally find an object fastened by a resistant piece of chain or wire. If you are using a charter vessel it is possible to tug it off with a rope or chain attached to the boat, keeping well clear while this is happening and making sure it is well tied on.

Figure 161 Exploring a sunken aeroplane

Expedition Diving

Expedition Planning

Diving expeditions by their very nature extend the knowledge and limits of diving, often taking place in remote locations hitherto unexplored. Expeditions range in scope, time and ambition, but even those which take place in more familiar localities will still extend knowledge of the underwater terrain. The one determining factor which separates an expedition from a holiday is that the expedition has a definite purpose or goal. A successful expedition may, of course, seem like a good holiday so we should not completely separate the two.

Expeditions are devised with specific aims in mind. It may be a photographic record of a particular locality or perhaps a biological or archaeological survey. Whatever the aim, it is important that an understanding is gained about the stages an expedition will go through before it is successfully completed. A simple strategy would be to assume each expedition has three phases: planning, execution and the writing up and publication of results.

The aim of this section is to give advice on the planning stage. This is a vital area, as bad planning will ensure very poor results.

A variety of things will need careful thought when planning any expedition. The list includes general aims, the area of operations/exploration, accommodation, boats, catering, availability of compressed air, fuel, financing, management and leadership, numbers and level of experience of personnel, personal equipment to be carried, safety/availability of recompression facilities and transportation.

The aims of an expedition should be clearly defined at an early stage. It is important not to set a target which is impossible to reach, just as it is important not to set goals too easily achieved. Members of an expedition need to feel they are facing something of a challenge, and that there is something new around the corner. As mentioned above, common themes underlying many diving expeditions have something of a scientific nature and bias. Just as rewarding, however, are those expeditions whose prime purpose is to explore fresh areas for diving, perhaps new shipwrecks or remote islands. Scientific aims may well be part of the expedition, but not necessarily the prime objective.

Any expedition planning should define the parameters in terms of diving locations. It is important to be realistic and not try to be over-ambitious in this respect. Bad weather, mechanical breakdown and illness can all play a part in altering theoretical plans, and it is prudent to anticipate these eventualities. All expeditions should have bad weather alternative plans. The scope and extent of the diving areas will be influenced by time available, speed/cost of travel and the nature of the diving activity. An archaeological expedition, for example, may restrict its activities to one predetermined site, whereas a photographic survey of an area may take in many locations and dive sites.

Adequate accommodation is essential on all expeditions. Keeping good morale is the duty of any expedition leader, and to provide accommodation which is damp, cold or fly-infested is guaranteed to dampen the spirits. Everyone has their own perception of the minimum tolerable degree of comfort, so roughing it will not be everyone's idea of having a good time. There is a large range of accommodation available for expeditions, depending on whereabouts in the world you are. Such a list would include camping, caravans, self-catering cottages/chalets/houses/hostels, bed & breakfast in hotels/guesthouses to full board in hotels. Many expeditions rely on charter vessels with on-board accommodation. It is important that appropriate accommodation is chosen according to local circumstance. Choice may be limited in very remote areas, and it may be that camping is the only alternative. Camping in cooler latitudes needs careful consideration, as diving in cold water loses large amounts of body heat. Living in a tent is not the best way of regaining such heat, and if camping is unavoidable it is imperative that the very best thermal tents with sewn-in groundsheets are used. Another important consideration when camping is to have a communal mess/meeting tent where every member of the team can congregate. Good communication is vital, and a tent of this sort will allow the leader to keep everyone informed as well as providing a welcome, warm environment to relax in.

Boats are an integral part of many expeditions, and are necessary in many parts of the world as the only means of reaching remote locations. Live-on-board charter vessels resolve accommodation/compressed air needs and are an excellent diving vehicle. Care needs to be taken when choosing such a vessel both in terms of facilities it offers and the expertise/co-operative nature of the skipper. It is important to choose a boat which has the cruising range required for the diving target areas. The section on 'Diving From Charter Vessels' gives useful advice on choosing the right boat for a successful expedition. Many expeditions rely on using boats which are transportable on road trailers and are used from shore bases. While diving from such boats allows speed and flexibility, it also introduces other potential problems. The availability of fuel is an obvious consideration, as is the need to take comprehensive spares for both boats and engines.

Catering is another area which will affect the morale of the divers, depending on its success. Diving two or three times a day burns up a lot of calories, and the body needs replenishing with nourishing food. This is especially important in colder climates, where hot food is essential. If self-catering, the availability of fresh provisions is an important planning factor. If self-sufficient, dried and packaged food will reduce both weight and bulk.

Compressed air is another planning consideration, and unless one is diving from a charter vessel with an on-board compressor it needs to be provided by a portable compressor. Very few expeditions take place near to a commercial source of air, and even if they do, frequent trips to fill cylinders become a costly, time-consuming chore. A wise leader will always plan to take at least two portable compressors, together with a supply of filter materials and spares. Without air we cannot dive, and it is imperative that compressors are kept going.

Fuel supplies for compressors, boats and vehicles are best acquired locally, although in remote areas sufficient supply may have to be carried. It is prudent to carry some fuel as a safeguard against failure of local supplies. Fuel can be bought in bulk, but may prove awkward to handle, especially if provided in large containers.

Finances must be one of the main concerns in the planning phase of any expedition. Many expeditions will be self-financing, with expedition members paying a fee to cover all eventualities. Deposits from expedition members are essential, as they prove commitment to go and do not allow a member to drop out without any financial involvement.

Figure 163 Portable compressor

Figure 162 Good catering facilities are important

Expense can be cushioned, however, with successful requests for grant aid and/or sponsorship. The BSAC Jubilee Trust, for example, will grant money towards bona fide expeditions, generally of a scientific/archaeological nature. The Royal Geographical Society will also sponsor major expeditions with proven leaders and personnel who are genuinely planning to further geographical knowledge. Grants are awarded on the understanding that full reports of findings will be submitted to the organization lending the money. Sponsorship is worth pursuing, especially if the expedition guarantees to use a certain type of equipment. For example, a certain brand of outboard motor or food product. The expedition is obliged to promote the company as sponsors, to take good photographs of the equipment being used, and to co-operate with any post-expedition promotion. It costs little to ask reputable companies, and is well worth the effort during early expedition costing. A final word on financial planning for charter boats, if they are involved. On booking a boat it is normal to pay 25 per cent of the cost of hire, a further 50 per cent four weeks before departure and 25 per cent on departure.

Personnel need to be carefully chosen, depending on the aims of the expedition. A mix of qualified divers is often fruitful, as the less experienced can be further developed in their range of skills by the more experienced. For buddy-system diving it is best to confine total divers involved to even numbers. Large numbers take much more organizing, and a maximum of twelve is a sensible guideline. If using portable boats/engines and compressors, personnel should include people with the technical knowledge to maintain and repair such equipment. Photographic, archaeological and biological expeditions obviously need people who are competent in such fields. Persons with culinary skills are necessary where meals are provided on a self-catering basis. Although it is important to have key positions filled by such experts, expeditions should provide the opportunity for those without such knowledge or experience to gain it and any guide to personnel selection should bear this in mind.

It is the responsibility of each diver to provide suitable personal equipment for the expedition. If diving a remote location, advice should be given about providing spares for equipment such as torches, masks and fins. Spare seals for dry suits, when used, are a useful item. Polythene storage bins give good protection against the rigours of a long journey in difficult terrain.

Safety of divers and safe diving procedures should always be uppermost in the mind of the expedition leaders and dive marshals. This is especially true in remote locations which may be hours, even days away from suitable recompression facilities. Decompression sickness in this situation could be disastrous, and careful planning of acceptable diving procedures is essential. Approved oxygen equipment for decompression accidents is a vital part of the expedition equipment to be carried.

Figure 164 Preparing and cleaning underwater photographic equipment

Transportation

Transportation probably takes the lion's share of the costs involved in expedition planning, and different options need to be considered and carefully weighed up before final decisions are taken.

The type of transport needed depends on the location and the type of expedition being undertaken. Diving expeditions cover a wide range of operations and locations and may vary between the exploration of a distant tropical island archipelago, hitherto unexplored underwater, to an archaeological or photographic survey in an area much closer to home. For the former it may be necessary to charter aircraft so as to be within reach of the nearest port, whereas the latter location may be very well served with regular passenger ferries and generally available charter vessels.

Diving expeditions, by their very nature, involve the transportation of many items of bulky, heavy equipment ranging from diving cylinders to tents, compressors to boats. Whenever air transport is the only viable method of transport, costs escalate. Such weighty and bulky items cannot be economically transported, but part of expedition planning must be to seek out alternatives. For example, examine the costs and possibility of hiring heavy items of equipment nearer the site of operations, so that only the divers and their personal equipment need to be transported. Commercial airline baggage weight limits are invariably inadequate for diving equipment plus personal luggage, but it may be possible to negotiate with the airlines beforehand to permit excess weight to be carried without incurring excess baggage costs. A sympathetic ear may be forthcoming if the airline in question would be mentioned in any expedition publicity, and it is worth enquiring whether they would value such a limited sponsorship arrangement. Even when all equipment has to be transported by air, it may be worth examining the possibilities of reduced baggage rates in exchange for publicity.

The use of surface travel will invariably be cheaper when it is a realistic option, even if more time consuming. It is still expensive, however, to take vehicles and trailers on commercial ferries, especially when travelling in the peak holiday period. You should question whether you need all the vehicles in your group at the final destination, as some may be left at the ferry port for collection on the return journey. Sometimes transport to ferry people about can be hired more cheaply at the location. If this is not possible then economic use of trailers should be considered. When using inflatable boats it may be possible to tow two on one trailer, in piggy-back fashion, with outboard motors stowed safely inside. Outboard motors are expensive items of equipment, however, and on long journeys need securing efficiently. The power-head should be kept elevated above the gearbox in order that unwanted oils, etc., do not contaminate the

Figure 165 Dive bags account for a great deal of room

Figure 166 Diving cylinders should be transported carefully

cylinder block. A useful means of achieving this, and at the same time providing protection from the impacts of a road journey, is to rest the powerhead on an old tyre. Inflatable boats, including RIBs, can' suffer substantial damage from rope chafing if incorrect knots are used for lashing them to a trailer. It can be possible for a brand-new boat to gain a hole in the side tube before it goes in the water, just from being towed several hundred miles with an incorrectly tied knot. The 'lorry driver's hitch' is the only fail-safe knot for this purpose. A much better idea than rope and more idiot proof is a system employing straps of the same dimensions and material as car seat-belt straps. With specially designed brackets (see Figure 168) they can be removed when the boat is being launched, and can be easily tightened with the non-slip buckles. (See Figure 167.)

Other heavy items of equipment can sometimes be carried using boats as trailers, but care must be taken not to exceed local laws regarding maximum weights for towed trailers. For trailers without brakes it is often unlawful, and certainly unwise, to exceed a trailer load of

half the unladen towing vehicle's kerbside weight.

Longer expeditions, involving a charter boat, can often swap crews by one team leaving with the boat and then meeting the second team at a prearranged location half-way through. The divers from the first team then drive the road vehicles back, while the second team return with the boat.

Figure 167 Quick release strap buckles

Figure 168 Load straps fixed to a boat trailer

Running Expeditions

The art of running successful expeditions is all about effective leadership and management. It is worth spending a little time in listing the qualities which make an effective leader, for without such a person expeditions will be less than happy events.

The leader will be an experienced diver who is fully conversant with the diving style and associated skills needed on the expedition in question. Above all the leader needs to be able to handle the multiplicity of personalities under his charge and inspire confidence in all of them. This will bring out and maximize the talents of all in the party, and make each person feel part of the project.

It is too easy for the shy and retiring person to be submerged in the hustle and bustle of a busy expedition. A successful leader of an expedition involving amateur divers will rarely succeed by being dictatorial or engendering a strictly military atmosphere. Key decisions do have to be made, but such decisions, if they are the correct ones, will be based on common sense and will have been taken following consultation, albeit of an informal nature. Good leaders are good communicators, both with those under their charge and with those with whom they have to deal on behalf of the expedition, for example charter-boat skippers. Successful expeditions are those in which all participants are kept up to date on current and future plans, and where decisions are explained to them. People can accept unpalatable decisions if they have understood the logic behind them. A successful leader will liaise with the charter-boat skipper and mutually agree diving plans, both for fair and foul weather. Such a leader has the confidence to delegate his authority to those in the party competent enough to carry out the tasks. A well-known adage states that the art of leadership is delegation, and it is certainly true that no single person can carry out every major role in a successful expedition. Above all the leader must lead by enthusiasm and example. Enthusiasm is infectious, as is gloom.

Running expeditions can be neatly divided into two specific areas: the actual diving/recording of events and the ancillary activities which are necessary to ensure decent living standards and successful diving. The running of diving activities is perhaps the most important aspect of any diving expedition. The leader is responsible for organizing realistic, enjoyable diving* plans which give ample opportunity for members to maximize their diving at the same time as staying well within the parameters of safety. This is especially true in remote locations where recompression/hospital facilities may be non-existent or many hours' travel away. If diving is from a charter boat, plans can only be made after consultation and agreement with the skipper, due regard being given to tides or other local conditions. A useful aid is to provide members of the expedition with a chart of the area. This allows them to study the terrain, and means that they are more comprehensively briefed.

A useful exercise is to hold a briefing meeting at the start of each day. This is very important to establish the objectives in the day's diving, and allows the dive marshal to plan without unnecessary duplication of tasks. It also allows the leader to check on any health/fitness to dive problems within the group and to answer any questions. It is all part of the communication process.

Part of the expedition leader's delegation of authority is to choose competent dive marshals for each day's diving, who may in turn appoint deputies to help them. If small boats are being used the dive marshal will choose a cox for each boat to be responsible for checking safety equipment, loading, fuel, launch and retrieval, etc.

The dive marshal of the day is responsible for buddy pairing, site location, perhaps in liaison with the boat skipper, dive plans, decompression practices and accurate record-keeping. It will be the responsibility of the marshal for the day to update the expedition log and to co-ordinate any discoveries made and the observations of individual divers. A debrief at the end of the diving day is a useful forum for gaining such information.

The dive marshal is obviously a key figure and must be chosen with care. Experienced divers would be chosen for this role, but opportunities should not be missed to allow the less experienced the chance to enhance their organizational skills. The latter would be supervised at all times in this key area of diving activities.

Figure 169 Dive boats preparing to get underway

The introduction of the BSAC '88 decompression tables and the increased use of variable profile decompression computers means that more than two dives per day may be possible under suitable conditions. The physiology of diving, however, remains the same and during a period involving diving every day, as expedition diving invariably is, a requirement is careful monitoring of all dives. Individuals should be encouraged to record accurately all dive details, whether they are diving with tables or computers. The dive marshal must also keep an accurate record. Deep repetitive diving should be avoided and it may be considered prudent to have the occasional day off from diving or, failing that, staying shallow for a day.

Expeditions from boats give the opportunity to teach divers good diving practice in terms of kitting and de-kitting economically without annoying others. Diving equipment expands to the space allotted, and it is useful to ask all members to acquire their own 'personal' piece of the deck to get changed in, to stow equipment once it has been removed and not to leave pieces strewn over the deck.

It is fairly easy to make a list of the routine duties which are usually common to all expeditions, whether they be boat or land based. Such activities would include cooking and washing up, cylinder filling, compressor maintenance, shopping for fresh food and fuelling/oiling outboard motors. Extra activities which may be a part of charter-boat expeditions could include spells of steering the boat, tending ropes and winches and overnight anchor watches. Not all the above, of course, will apply to every expedition, as in some parts of the world boats are crewed by professional crew, meals cooked by a professional cook and divers may not be welcome at the wheel or even on the bridge!

Whatever the situation, it is unlikely the expedition will succeed without some sort of rota system, however informal this may be.

In all groups of people there tend to be those who are willing to work hard and volunteer for jobs. There are others who may wish to exploit this keenness and generally try to avoid the more unsociable and less pleasant jobs. It is not everyone's idea of fun to fill a dozen cylinders in the dark and cold at the end of a hard day's diving, to be dragged from a warm bunk at two in the morning to watch for 'traffic' while anchored at sea or to be incarcerated in a small, hot galley while the boat heaves about in a Force 5 wind. Without someone doing these jobs, however, everything else falls apart. The wise leader will anticipate all such tasks, and will put together a jobs rota in advance. This will allow him to place people with specific skills to a particular job, e.g., compressor maintenance, but will also allow him a global view of the expedition time slot, with a view to building in variety. One does not want to hear complaints such as 'I filled all the cylinders yesterday and the day before' or 'Why is it always me getting up to do anchor watch in the middle of the night?' A successful leader is seen to be fair with the allocation and rotation of jobs.

Catering is one of the key areas in any expedition. Many charter boats have their own cook aboard, and this task is not the responsibility of the divers. Shore-based expeditions may also take along their own cook. Where cooking is the responsibility of the expedition members it is important to provide food which is nourishing, tasty and at the same time does not require hours of preparation. A menu can often be supplemented by fresh fish and shellfish, but it is important that the supply of this is controlled to avoid wastage. It is all too easy to catch dozens of fish when a few will suffice. Expeditions rarely have the means to keep fresh food for longer than a day or two, and there is nothing worse than the smell of decaying fish, especially in a hot climate.

One of diving's creature comforts comes in the form of a warm drink once the dive is over, especially in cool-water areas of the world. This should form part of the jobs rota.

Meals should be planned around the diving and not the other way round. Good practice, for digestive reasons, is to only have a drink and a light snack before the first dive of the day. A 'brunch' following the dive is much more appreciated, as appetites are sharpened and a meal helps restore calories and body heat.

Between the dives most expedition members will want to explore any islands or other sights, and time needs to be built into the programme to allow this to happen. This is especially important if the expedition lives in the cramped confines of a charter boat where nerves can become edgy.

Finally, it is very important that the results of any day's diving are recorded while memories are fresh. A surface and underwater photographic record of any expedition is a priority area, both to satisfy any sponsors and to present the expedition at conferences/meetings, etc., after the event. The increased use of video has an important role here in recording events as they happen.

At the conclusion of any expedition someone should be tasked with producing the expedition report as professionally as possible. Such reports help tremendously when attempting to organize and gain support for future expeditions.

Figure 170 Preparing to enter the water from a charter vessel

Diving Remote Locations

Remote diving locations, by definition, involve divers in a high degree of self-sufficiency and forward planning, yet potentially they provide some of the most exciting diving available.

Defining what constitutes a remote location is not clear-cut. A large, well-equipped charter vessel may travel hundreds of kilometres from 'civilization', whereas 40 kilometres is stretching the limit for modern RIBs. A reasonable definition of a remote location is an area not normally dived routinely because of its distance from civilization and its subsequent difficulty of access, or because it lies on the limits of the mode of transport used to travel there.

This section is designed to highlight the special equipment, technique and safety aspects of diving in remote, rarely dived areas of the world.

Equipment

It is particularly important, for obvious reasons, that equipment for boats, compressors and outboard motors needs to be in excellent working order before travelling to areas where no spares or maintenance can be acquired. Comprehensive lists of spares need to be carried for all equipment vital to the boat's operation and to diving activities. Personal equipment needs to be checked thoroughly before departure and where necessary serviced. Dry-suit repair materials, spare 'O' rings for cylinder valves and torches, spare batteries for torches, etc., are all essential parts of the divers' equipment when self-help is the order of the day.

Due to the reduced presence of the usual rescue services, equipment which limits the risk of losing surface contact with divers will become very important. 'Day-Glo' hoods are fairly essential, as are large, visible SMBs in certain conditions. Many divers now carry collapsible fluorescent flags, which can be held aloft in order to attract the attention of observers in the boat. Wise expedition leaders may well decide to provide all expedition members with comprehensive equipment lists, and perhaps organize spares or equipment which can be easily shared in order to save space and weight.

If boats are being used, it is essential that they carry a good marine-band radio capable of transmitting and receiving on the essential channels in use over the area where diving activities are carried out. Land-based expeditions need an equivalent radio capable of contacting help if required. A spare radio is a useful addition in case of breakdown.

Figure 171 Remote island

Figure 172 A tropical island can constitute a remote diving location

In many parts of the world electronic navigation systems provide an accurate means of finding diving locations from boats and for giving accurate position fixes. In areas where signal strength is weak or where no coverage is available, then alternative methods of navigation need to be used. The increased use and greater availability of satellite navigation systems will really open up the globe to dive boats seeking to explore new areas. Excellent accuracy is achievable, and their full potential has still to be realized.

A standard first-aid kit, as described in the BSAC diving manual *Sport Diving*, is insufficient when diving well away from medical help. Many expeditions have as part of their personnel doctors or para-medics who are qualified to administer drugs or give injections. Large well-funded expeditions may well have a resident doctor capable of dealing with minor surgery. Good advice, when in remote areas, would be to carry the most comprehensive first-aid kit possible, including oxygen. More than one person must be qualified to administer 100 per cent oxygen to divers suffering symptoms of decompression sickness. Diving in remote locations will inevitably mean many hours of delay in reaching recompression facilities, and the use of oxygen in such situations may mean the difference between full recovery or life in a wheelchair.

Technique and safety

Divers in remote locations must be aware of their isolation and lack of reliance on other boats/diving parties. Dive planning and execution is particularly important for these reasons, and the old saying of 'Plan the dive and dive the plan' becomes very important.

Divers may have to deal with unknown tidal streams or waves higher than normally experienced. In such conditions, experienced boathandlers are essential. When observing divers from a charter vessel you can take advantage of the height of the boat, but diving from such boats will often involve the use of an inflatable tender. The worst thing that can happen in these circumstances is for divers to be swept away by the tide, unseen by those on the boat. Experienced boathandlers will take observation positions, avoiding looking into the sun, especially when it is low in the sky. The divers themselves need to be well briefed in terms of agreed dive times and safe areas in which to surface. SMBs may well be essential equipment where there is any possibility of divers being swept away. The large torpedo type in an orange or red fluorescent colour is perhaps the most visible. Submersible strobe lights are readily available, and could prove particularly useful as a means of locating divers on the surface in dark or poor light conditions.

Finally, be very aware of the risks of decompression sickness, which will be amplified by the remoteness of the diving area. Avoid periods of deep repetitive diving, diving when tired, or suffering from the effects of alcohol. Careful recording of depth, time, and surface interval is an obvious requirement. At all times remember that a good diver is not one who can get out of trouble, but one who avoids it altogether.

Figure 173 Oxygen equipment is essential for remote diving locations

Figure 174 Tender for charter vessel

Diving From Charter Vessels

There is no doubt that the use of charter vessels has opened up whole new diving areas and, in many parts of the world, has made possible exploration in its truest sense. In the United Kingdom it has been traditional to use a mixture of inflatables/RIBS and larger vessels, and it is probably true to say that we have been somewhat slow in catching up on the delights and ease of diving which charter vessels allow.

It is useful to divide the subject of diving from charter vessels into the following sections:

1. Types of charter vessels and the equipment they carry
2. Diving techniques
3. Advantages of such diving
4. Choosing a boat/skipper and running a successful charter

There is no doubt that there is a vast range of vessels which could be brought under the title of 'charter', ranging from the large fishing coble, more used to taking out sea anglers, to the purpose-built vessel with every on-board creature comfort imaginable. Whereas the former is used as a substitute for private small boats, on a daily basis, with a limited range of facilities, the latter opens up the possibility of long-range cruising to remote locations without the need to return to port each evening.

Our classification can begin with the day vessel. Regardless of where it is in the world, this vessel will have no accommodation aboard for the divers, but will have all the facilities required for a comfortable day at sea. These will include compressed air or spare cylinders, a dive ladder, radar and navigation equipment/depth sounder, shelter from the sun or rough weather, and a simple galley for lunchtime refreshments. A useful addition is an inflatable tender which can be used to cover divers in the water, or to ferry people and equipment when required.

The weekend vessel will have all the facilities of the day vessel, but will add simple, though adequate, accommodation facilities. One would expect an improved galley, possibly on a self-catering basis.

The week/fortnight vessel would ideally be between 15 and 20 metres in length. Morale on a trip of a week or longer is partly dependent on eating well, so one would expect a well-equipped galley for this purpose. Good-quality accommodation is essential, and the boat should have a minimum one-week endurance in food, water and fuel. It should be capable of a speed of 7 knots in winds of Force 4–5. It will have all the other facilities of the types listed above.

The extended cruise vessel is the best equipped of all charters. There are relatively few available, and many are custom-built with a very comprehensive galley. Accommodation will be in cabins with washbasins. The boat may be fitted with stabilizers and should have a two-week minimum endurance in food, water and fuel. It should be capable of at least 10 knots in Force 4–5 winds. One would expect extensive electronic navigation equipment, which could include side-scan sonar. Deck facilities may include a small laboratory for photographic processing or biological analysis.

While more and more small boats are carrying increasingly sophisticated equipment in terms of electronic navigation and wreck finding, the charter vessel has for years given divers the opportunity of experiencing these advantages. While it takes years to become a competent skipper of a charter vessel, in a relatively short time divers can become familiar with and confident in the use of the types of equipment found in the wheelhouse.

Small boats are wet boats, and there is nothing like the shelter of the charter vessel to make familiarization with

Figure 175 Inside a well-equipped charter vessel

Decca Navigator, radar and depth sounders a more comfortable experience. Many charter vessels have facilities for working with charts, often with a purpose-built table. Used in conjunction with electronic navigation equipment and depth sounders, they are a valuable aid in finding hitherto unknown sites and can open up a whole new diving world.

The techniques for diving from charter vessels are somewhat specialized, but common sense ought to be the underlying theme. There are three phases: the entry, the dive itself, and re-entry into the charter vessel.

It is vital that some efficient liaison system with the skipper is built into any dive plan. Fatalities have occurred in the past when divers have jumped off the boat at the wrong time to be swept into a still-turning prop. The entry phase is therefore vital and needs good co-ordination within the diving team.

Ideally, the divers should be split into two groups ('waves'), thereby creating less congestion when kitting up and allowing those not diving to assist those who are. This will also ensure adequate surface dive marshalling.

Timing can be important, particularly in parts of the world with tidal waters, when slack water windows are vital ingredients to a successful dive. In this situation it is likely that all divers will need to enter the water over a relatively short time period, making it impossible to split into two diving waves. Kitting up can be awkward in this situation, especially with divers who do not do it in a logical order or who have not learnt the discipline of a tidy equipment bag. Inexperienced divers may have their equipment strewn around the deck or put on their fins before donning a diving cylinder in a rolling sea.

Even though all divers enter the water in the same wave, they will do so at intervals as most boats only enable one or two to jump in simultaneously. Unless divers go in at reasonable intervals, they will all surface together and the skipper will find himself having to pick everyone up at once. As larger boats may lack manoeuvrability, this could present a problem.

A lot of charter vessels have a gate in the gunwale which allows only one diver through at a time. Many of the divers in a group will be regular buddies and will be used to each other's kitting-up speed. There is little point in planning to make the slowest the first to enter the water unless they are told in good time that they should start to get ready. Good kitting-up technique will ensure that all equipment is together before they start, as only limited space is available. Weightbelts are often stored together in a locker or box, and there is nothing more annoying than a diver at one end of the boat having to stagger under the encumbrance of all his equipment past everyone else in order to retrieve one.

The actual entry to the water will require the vessel to slow down, place the engine in neutral, and approach the site, often marked with a weighted shotline and buoy, as slowly and precisely as possible. Many vessels require the divers to jump feet first from the deck at the signal given. Skippers will give this command once the engine is in neutral. In some parts of the world greater comfort is achieved using a stern diving platform, almost at water level, which divers merely step off. The 'dive barge' or 'flat top' used in many tropical locations gives easy access to the sea due to the low point of entry and good use of space on the boat.

Once the divers have safely entered the water, the skipper should be notified.

The dive itself needs to be covered from the charter vessel, and this can be an exacting task if up to twelve divers are in the water at the same time. Surface marker buoys can be useful in this situation, and are essential if there is any danger of the divers moving away from a fixed dive site. Sometimes the skipper will send out a crew member in the inflatable tender to cover the divers and to assist with the removal of ancillary equipment once they surface. During the dive it is important that the dive records are kept up to date. If all divers are in the water together, a member of the crew should be given this responsibility.

Figure 176 Entering from a charter vessel

Picking up the divers directly into the charter vessel is generally easier via a suitable ladder. The ladder needs to allow divers to climb aboard wearing fins, and perhaps the most efficient design is shown in Figure 177. After climbing back onto the vessel with all equipment the divers can de-kit with all their equipment at hand. Many skippers prefer divers to climb back into the accompanying inflatable tender as this does not require manoeuvring the large boat several times. This has some disadvantages, as much equipment is heaped into perhaps only one inflatable, together with the divers. This load has then to be transferred back to the larger boat, and anyone who has tried this in even a moderate sea will understand the problems. The inflatable falls as the large boat rises, and two or three hands are needed to keep it alongside. Equipment can easily be dropped whilst being passed across, and then usually ends up scattered across the deck. This is not an efficient method of re-entry and is only recommended when the divers surface in an area too shallow or hazardous to allow the charter vessel to pick them up.

Skippers have their own methods of diver pick-up, and part of the charter leader's responsibility is to find out how your individual likes things done. In the water, the divers should be alert and stay close together. They will be signalled when it is their turn to be picked up. It is often better to remain stationary and let the boat come to you. A large boat only has one chance of getting close, and if you attempt to swim towards it you may be obscured by the prow. Skilful skippers will almost stop when you are opposite the ladder, and some use prop wash to blow divers onto the ladder. Only one person can climb up at once, so the diver waiting should keep a firm hold of the ladder or a fender whilst waiting. Once you are on the ladder the boat will drift in neutral until you are safely aboard. A clear message to the skipper that the divers are clear is necessary at this point.

The advantages of diving from charter vessels are obvious to those who have had experience. The possibility of exploring remote locations, the minimum of logistical problems, compressed air on tap, the opportunity to climb out of a diving suit, the comfort of cabins and sheltered spaces on deck, the availability of food and drinks, all contribute to a relatively effortless manner of diving. Added to these, as mentioned above, are the opportunities to improve seamanship and navigational skills. Anyone who has dived using small boats will agree that most of the effort and energy is spent actually getting to the dive site.

The disadvantages on a well-run charter and a well-equipped boat are very few. Seasickness can be a problem with some individuals, as there may well be no respite from a rolling sea. Most people, however, acquire their 'sea legs' after a day or two. If anchoring is necessary at sea the team members should work out an anchor watch system, which can prove tiring. Being dragged from a warm bunk at two o'clock in the morning is not everyone's idea of having a good time! One important detail which needs to be taken into account is the possibility of charging torch or photographic equip-

Figure 177 Returning aboard via the diving ladder

ment batteries. This will be particularly important if the trip is longer than a day or two.

The key to all successful charters is picking the right boat and skipper. The importance of the skipper cannot be stressed enough, as this factor can make or break any diving expedition. The ideal skipper is one who owns the vessel and who is also a diver. The latter means he understands the sport, its techniques, and its constraints. The fact that he owns the vessel means that if he wants his customers to return he has got to run an enjoyable trip. Unfortunately, too many skippers are employees who sometimes lose interest after a season or two and then try to make life easy for themselves at the expense of the paying customer. This will often manifest itself with an excuse to return to the safe haven of a particular harbour. Mythical storms, or forecasts of bad weather, are favourite excuses which are used to run back to a favourite bar and groups of friends.

A leader of any group of divers chartering a boat must understand that the skipper is ultimately responsible for the safety of the boat and its occupants and cannot be expected to put either at risk. The planning stage of any charter must include a sensible itinerary of cruising and diving. Fair and foul weather plans must be evolved, and one must remember that the skipper also has to sleep and eat. After diving all day, you cannot expect a night passage to another remote location. The best charters tend to have a good balance between diving and exploring new locations. In the planning stage it is prudent to work on the average speed of the vessel and determine how far it is possible to steam, and allow dives to take place on the way. In the past many divers have expected to dive remote locations, and then grumble because they spend all day travelling without a dive.

It is vital at the start of the charter that the leader discusses and agrees his plan with the skipper. At this stage it is important to acquire the routines on board and, if necessary, draw up a job rota to share the load. Little things like this help the smooth running of the charter, and ensure that people do not feel they are taking the lion's share of, for example, cylinder filling. Some vessels, of course, have all such domestic tasks done by crew members. A list of the hot drinks preferences of all aboard is useful. A simple matrix with personnel names down the side and variations of tea/coffee with/without sugar, etc., across the top and a tick in the appropriate place is an efficient way of organizing this.

While the skipper is ultimately responsible for the safety of the vessel and all aboard, the diving organization is the responsibility of the leader, after liaison with the skipper. The exception to this would be diving organized by commercial schools/shops.

As leader you need to be aware of any additional problems, e.g., lack of easily available recompression facilities, if diving remote locations and to ensure good dive discipline whilst on charter.

A successful charter needs a good boat and crew as well as an amiable skipper. Many boats are excellent in all respects. Others, however, may not meet the required standards and should be avoided. Horror stories exist of leaking cabins, continually blocked toilets, filthy galleys and inedible food. Fortunately, these vessels become well known very quickly and the news spreads. There is nothing to beat a word-of-mouth recommendation from those who have been aboard, particularly if you are unsure of a boat's pedigree.

Figure 178 A typical charter vessel

Diving Overseas

One of the difficulties for the British diver in diving overseas is the journey. In the jet age travelling to exotic places is achievable by many people. The problem for the diver is that the weight limits imposed by airlines make it difficult to take diving equipment and the normal accoutrements of a holiday overseas. Some compromise has to be made, though this is often at the expense of a non-diving travelling companion's baggage allowance.

The really weighty items such as cylinder and weight-belt can usually be hired at the destination, or within surface transport range if the site is very remote. Divers consider mask, fins and snorkel as personal equipment and normally prefer to take these with them. This category is frequently extended to cover regulator and buoyancy compensator, on the grounds of familiarity equating with safety. A locally hired regulator may well lack the direct feed fitting for your buoyancy compensator and is very unlikely to sport an octopus mouthpiece.

Many British divers now use dry suits and those who prefer the membrane version have a weight advantage when travelling to overseas venues demanding such thermal protection. There are a surprising number of seas, climates or seasons where a UK diving suit can be worn comfortably or even advantageously. This particularly goes for areas of the Mediterranean in the winter months, though care may have to be exercised, when out of the water, not to overheat.

For many overseas venues a thin 4 millimetre wet suit of the type favoured by water skiers and wind surfers can be most appropriate, though many British divers resort to their UK pool suit in such waters. As the water temperature rises, the prime purpose of the dive suit changes. It becomes more necessary to protect the diver from coral grazes and stings than heat loss. For this reason many divers based in the tropics wear overalls rather than a conventional dive suit; but apart from being effective, available and cheap, overalls are not an ideal diving garment. Problems have arisen because they are so loose fitting and some types will also tend to trap air and cause buoyancy difficulties. Far more glamorous are the stretch Lycra skin-tight suits now fashionable in much of the Pacific dive scene. These have the advantage of being very lightweight and easy to pack and are at least as streamlined as the diver's body under water. Depending on the body they enclose, Lycra suits are much more glamorous on the holiday video and may be a slimming incentive for some divers!

Figure 179 Membrane drysuit

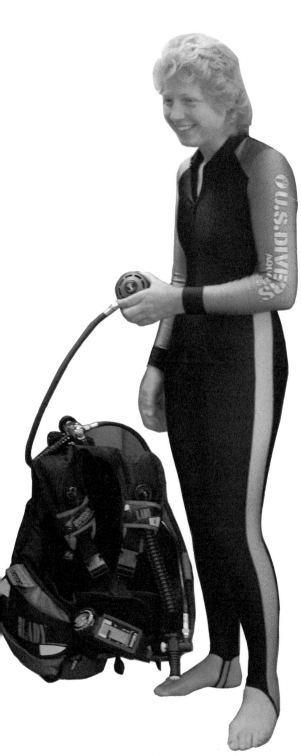

Figure 180 Lycra skin tight – for tropical waters

Figure 181 Dive shop for tuition and diving trips

Figure 182 Diving equipment for hire and repair

Decompression computers come into the category of equipment to be taken and for many it is important that they travel with the diver in the aircraft cabin. This is so they can accurately monitor the pressure changes experienced by the diver throughout the flight and thus properly reflect the tissue gas levels when diving commences. Most baggage travels in non-pressurized holds and therefore experiences quite different pressures, as many divers packing mechanical depth gauges in their dive bags have discovered to their cost.

Some airlines can occasionally be sweet talked into increasing the weight allowance for divers, but this is unusual. It is well worth packing underwater photographic equipment in a strong but lightweight case of suitable dimensions so that it can be carried as cabin baggage. This also should mean it is safe from the ravages of the baggage handling system.

Whilst most security systems are classified as 'film safe', if film stock has to undergo many checks the effects can be accumulative. Some of the older equipment is definitely not film safe and permission should be sought to have film hand-checked. In many of the more exotic venues films and video cassettes are not readily available, so suitable quantities should be taken.

In most cases the diver overseas will be using a commercial outlet of some kind in order to go diving. This may be a simple arrangement of cylinder or weightbelt hire, or boat hire, or may be a total involvement with a diving school. Whichever option is followed, it is probable that at some stage a verification will be made of the diver's qualification level or diving skills. This could be as cursory as a glance at a CMAS card or as detailed as a check-out dive with an instructor.

Practical experience shows that a BSAC Qualification Record Book, supported by a dive log showing the most recent dives made, is the most universally accepted proof of diving ability. BSAC/CMAS (World Underwater Federation) cards may be purchased from BSAC HQ if photocopies of appropriate QRB pages are submitted.

The organization of diving in most countries is on a far more commercial footing than the British club-oriented style. Many divers overseas will do all their diving through a school, often only on one or two holidays per year. Even when relatively experienced, it is common for them to dive with an instructor or guide from the school. It is common for a guide to lead a group of four or five customers and you can expect to be placed within such a group, rather than being allowed to dive as a buddy pair.

In places where the BSAC system and qualifications are better understood, organized British groups may be able to negotiate management of their own dives. This means they can dive in a style they are more familiar with, even when sharing facilities such as a hard boat with other divers. All this will be a matter for diplomatic negotiation by the party leader and such discussions can often be held before the trip takes place.

Whether diving with a familiar buddy or in a guided group of strangers, there will be many dive features quite different to UK dives. After all, that is one of the purposes of visiting the area! Almost certainly, different equipment will be used, even if it is just a strange cylinder and different protective clothing. This will probably mean a change in weight requirements. A word of warning – British divers are renowned world wide for their love of too much lead! Try and dispel that belief by carefully choosing just the right amount for neutral buoyancy throughout the dive.

If your cylinder has an unfamiliar valve, learn how it operates; many overseas divers use reserve levers rather than a contents gauge. If you have your own regulator and contents gauge with you it may be preferable to commence the dive with the reserve pulled and use your contents gauge as normal. Be sure that your dive leader understands the situation and agree a contents level at which you will give the 'I am on reserve' signal. Make doubly sure when diving with unknown companions that you have an agreed set of signals before starting the dive; it is too late to develop

Figure 183 Dive computer in an aircraft cockpit

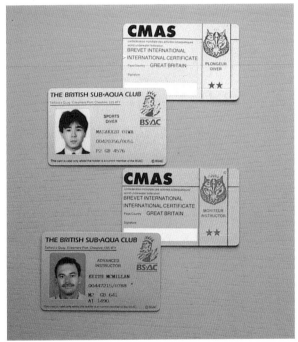

Figure 184 Reserve valve

Figure 185 BSAC qualification record book and log book

Figure 186 BSAC/CMAS diver and instructor cards

these at the bar later. Check that you understand and can correctly operate any other hired equipment, such as buoyancy devices and weightbelt.

Diving in a guided group involves different techniques to our buddy system. The instructor may choose to lead from the front, or may control sheepdog style from behind the group. In either case a more experienced member of the group may be asked to assist by acting as 'tail-end Charlie', or group pilot, as appropriate. Good practice is for the instructor to lead the descent and final ascent so as to be in the best position for control.

British divers often suffer 'vision narcosis' – they are overwhelmed by the underwater visibility and light levels. Divers used to the signals of limited visibility and darkness to indicate increasing depth are too easily seduced to greater-than-planned-for depths. The basic laws of physiology and physics affect the diver regardless of the visibility and warmth. Nitrogen narcosis is just as likely in tropical waters, however its symptoms may well be subtly changed by the diver's different feelings about the water conditions.

Remember that many of the exotic life forms you will meet are used to fighting for survival. If a fish does not flee from you this may well be because it feels its poisonous spines are an adequate defence. Before diving, it is worth looking at pictures of the more harmful forms of marine life you might encounter. The local dive shop or school will usually assist you in this matter and also advise you on the damage you might do to the underwater environment. Careless finning and inadequate buoyancy adjustment, especially from would-be photographers, does a tremendous amount of damage to coral reefs.

Be aware that many reef sites are under great ecological threat and it is often forbidden to take anything other than photographs. Laws on removing souvenirs from shipwrecks are also frequently very strictly enforced. An expensive extended stay – courtesy of the local legal system – is not an ideal end to an overseas holiday, so be sensitive to such rules.

Information on overseas diving venues is frequently published in *Diver* magazine and some information may also be obtained from BSAC HQ. Having dived a particular area you may well be able to submit a report to BSAC HQ to update or expand the data held there.

Do not expect all overseas sites to look like a film set; there is as much variety in underwater scenery as on land. Many British divers have been amazed at the amount of life in the 'dead' Mediterranean, once they have adjusted to the different lifeforms, colours and scale. Equally, do not be disappointed if eventually you find your familiar Scottish shipwreck is still your favourite site – after all, it is probably more accessible!

Figure 187 Cone shell

Figure 188 Lion fish (*Ptevois volitaw*)

Figure 189 Exotic dive site – some marine life here may be used to fighting for survival!

Figure 190 Tropical island – divers should beware of nitrogen narcosis

HSE Regulations

Regulations relevant to diving activities in the United Kingdom laid down by the Health and Safety Executive (HSE) are of interest to amateur divers in the areas of diving instructional, scientific activities, and the testing of cylinders.

Following the poor safety record in North Sea diving activities during the oil boom of the 1970s the HSE were tasked with providing stricter codes of diving practice for all commercial diving activities. The result was the production and implementation of the 'Diving Operations at Work Regulations – 1981'. All professional diving activities come under the control of these regulations, which require all divers to have an extensive annual medical examination conducted by an 'approved' doctor, proof of training in a government-recognized school, and other mandatory controls. Strict controls are laid down for the conduct of diving operations, an example being the requirement for a fully staffed and operational recompression chamber available on site.

Most of the areas under the control of the above regulations are outside the domain of the amateur diver as amateur diving is not part of this legislation. There was clearly a need, however, to clarify the situation for instructors who gained financial reward for their teaching and for scientists who may include diving in their activities.

With the former in mind the BSAC pioneered the award of a Restricted HSE Part IV certificate for qualified instructors who had reached the grade of BSAC Advanced Instructor (CMAS 2 Star), or above. BSAC 1st Class Divers who are also BSAC Club Instructors (CMAS 1 Star) also qualified for Restricted Part IV status. This was purely for those who were involved in teaching diving; any other involvement in professional diving placed them under full HSE Regulations. Instructors registering under Part IV of the regulations are still required to undergo the above-mentioned medical examination annually, but are removed from the parts of the Regulations which are pertinent to open water commercial operations. It is worth noting that a Restricted Part IV certificate is only valid if the annual medical has been carried out. Since there is no checking procedure, should anything go wrong and the medical is found to be out of date, then the diver concerned is likely to be found in contravention of the regulations.

Scientific diving operations are exempt from the above Regulations under Exemption DOW 2/88 which exempts diving operations:

a. which are primarily for the purpose of scientific research and are carried out by scientific research workers who dive from time to time in the course of their work using self-contained underwater breathing apparatus and

b. in which no person at work dives to greater than 50m nor does his routine decompression time exceed 20 minutes and

c. which are carried out by, or on behalf of, or under the auspices of a national or government research institute, a university, a museum or other similar organization and

d. where a full diving team comprising persons with duties under the Regulations is not available.

It is important that amateur divers do not inadvertently break the law if they agree to perform tasks of work. Divers who agree to free a fouled boat propeller or lobster pots may do so in an effort to foster good diver/fisherman relations, but if they accept any money or goods in kind which exceed true expenses then they are breaking the law. If the fisherman offers a bottle of whisky worth £10 then the diver must prove £10 of expenses. It is often thought that if money is accepted but is paid into club funds, rather than to the individual, then the law is not broken. This is not true and has been likened to having an alteration done on the house with the builder asking not to be paid himself but to pay his mother-in-law!

HSE Regulations (Explosives Branch) pertaining to diving cylinders are as follows:

Air cylinders to the older specifications HOS, HOT, HOAL 1, 2 and 4 are no longer manufactured, but owners may continue to use them. Current HSE specifications for the UK are: Steel – BS 5045/1/CM/S and Aluminium – BS 5045/3. There is a current BSAC requirement for all cylinders, including ABLJ/BC cylinders to be tested no later than three years from new and then every two years. Cylinders should also be given an annual internal visual inspection.

It is likely that in the near future recommendations for testing will be amended as follows: All cylinders to be tested every four years with a recommended annual internal inspection. The test should be carried out in accordance with BS 5430 and divers are recommended to use test houses approved by the Inspectorate for Diving Equipment, Servicing and Testing (IDEST).

Salvage Laws

Anyone who has delved into the laws regarding salvage of wrecks will quickly confirm that such an experience brings home the maze that exists in this area. It explains, to a large extent, why so often the law is ignored by people who see the rules as discriminating against the salvor with no realistic reward for the financial risk and effort required in a salvage operation. This section is intended for general guidance. Those looking for precise legal definition should consult 'Halsbury's Laws of England, Volume 35, Shipping and Navigation'.

The first principle to understand is that all wrecks/ wreckage belong to someone and that legally you should make every effort to trace the owner before removing anything.

The second principle is that anything found on a wreck or in the sea must be reported to the Receiver of Wreck at the nearest customs house.

If you have found a wreck, it will probably have occurred fairly recently. If the ship and its cargo were covered by insurance, the claim for total loss will more than likely have been paid and the rights will therefore belong to the underwriters concerned. It may then be possible to purchase the rights in that wreck and her cargo for a nominal sum. Lloyd's will probably help trace the underwriters, or, in the case of a war casualty, the Board of Trade, War Risk Insurance Office may be able to help.

Before deciding to acquire a particular wreck you should seriously consider whether it may constitute a hazard to navigation. If your wreck causes damage to another vessel you will be held responsible, and this could prove to be very costly.

Having concluded an agreement with the underwriters or owners you may begin salvage operations. You should first notify the appropriate lighthouse authority, and then give some consideration to the Merchant Shipping Act of 1894, the law which governs modern salvage.

Section 518 of the Act reads:

Where any person finds or takes possession of any wreck within the limits of the United Kingdom he shall –
a If he is the owner thereof, give notice to the receiver of the district stating that he has found or taken possession of the same and describing the marks by which the same may be recognized;
b if he is not the owner thereof, as soon as possible deliver the same to the receiver of the district: and if any person fails without reasonable cause to comply with this section, he shall, for each offence, be liable to a fine not exceeding £100 and shall in addition, if he is not the owner, forfeit any claim to salvage and shall be liable to pay to the owner of the wreck if it is claimed, or if it is unclaimed to the person entitled to same, double the value thereof to be recovered in the same way as a fine or a like amount under the Act.

The Act has to decide exactly what is wreck, and this includes jetsam, flotsam, lagan and derelicts found in or on the shores of the sea or any tidal water. Jetsam covers all objects which have been thrown overboard from a ship to lighten her; flotsam those which remain afloat after a ship has sunk; and lagan articles which have been thrown overboard attached to a buoy or marker. A derelict is a vessel that has been abandoned.

If the owner of a wreck found in the UK and held by a receiver fails to establish possession, it can be disposed of. The salvors will receive expenses from the sale, the amount determined by the Board of Trade. Wrecks can be claimed by their rightful owner after the payment of all expenses, costs, fees and salvage.

All this can prove to be rather daunting to the amateur diver. Having acquired your wreck, as the legal owner there is nothing to stop you removing it piece by piece. Strictly speaking, it is an offence to salve only part of a wreck, especially if, as mentioned above, you are unfortunate enough to sink another vessel.

History has shown that salvors only collect some 30 to 50 per cent of the value of the cargo, or the same percentage of the proceeds of the sale of the material recovered. When one adds this to the fact that there is no law which prevents diving the wreck (unless it comes under the Act protecting historic sites) and removing material, provided that it is declared to the Receiver of Wreck, we have a recipe for bending if not breaking the law. The rewards for doing things legally are so small that the temptation to break the law has been succumbed to many times over the years.

The only real protection afforded by the law to any wreck site came into being with the Protection of Wrecks Act, 1973. This Act enables the Secretary of State to designate by order the site of any wrecked vessel lying on or in the sea bed if he is satisfied that it ought to be protected from unauthorized interference on account of its historical, archaeological or artistic importance. A protection order identifies the site of the wreck and specifies the extent of the restricted area around it. Within that area, it is an offence without the authority of a licence granted by the Secretary of State, to tamper with, damage or remove any part of the wrecked vessel or anything contained or formerly contained in it, to carry out diving or salvage operations, to use diving or salvage equipment or to deposit materials so as to obliterate or obstruct access to the site or to damage the wreck. The intention to designate a site is given local and national press publicity and all applications for designation are decided by a committee of expert advisors under the chairmanship of Viscount Runciman of Doxford. This body is usually known as the Runciman Committee. Designated sites are usually marked with buoys and are clearly marked on Admiralty charts.

Index

Illustration Acknowledgements

Thanks are due to the following for allowing the use of copyright photographs:

Mike Busuttili, figures 88–90, 147–148, 153, 161; Adrian Clarke, figures 39, 184; Dick Clarke, figure 143; Brian Cumming, figure 38; Bernard Eaton, figures 3, 14, 43, 45, 47, 49–52, 64–65, 139, 141, 146, 164–165, 173, 181; Deric Ellerby, figure 183; Diver Magazine, figure 144; Helle Engineering Ltd, figure 123; Jerry Hazzard, figures 124, 163, 190; Mike Holbrook, figures 13, 68, 85, 98–100, 160, 166; Gordon Longworth, figures 1, 4, 7–9, 11, 62, 67, 162, 169–172; Kendal McDonald, figures 56–57; Rick Oldfield, figure 188; Rob Palmer FRGS, figures 131–133, 135–138; George Rowing, figures 84, 149, 177, 182, 189; Josef Ruprecht Aquazepp, figure 128; Dave Shaw, figures 6, 59–60, 61, 70–71, 86–90, 112–113, 117–121, 155, 158; Wes Skiles, figure 134; John Stubbs, figures 10, 48, 53, 63, 66, 75, 77–78, 122, 140, 141; Sub Sea Services, figure 179; David Swales, figure 180; Dave Whapshot, figures 157–159, 161; Barry Winfield, figures 167–168.

The photographs opening each section are by Mike Busuttili (Wreck Diving, Underwater Techniques), Adrian Clarke (Decompression), Bernard Eaton (Decompression Diving), Gordon Longworth (Dive Planning, Expedition Diving) and Rob Palmer (Specialist Diving).

All the artwork for this book was specially commissioned from Rico Oldfield.

The British Sub-Aqua Club would like to express its appreciation to the Maltese Department of Tourism, Air Malta and the Calypso Diving Centre on Gozo for their hospitality while taking a number of photographs contained in this Manual.